Main Street

Marketing

How Local Small Business Owners Can Get More Customers,

Skyrocket Their Profits, And Dominate Their Bigger Competitors

(Without Working 80 Hours A Week And Missing Their Son's Baseball

Games)

Tim Chermak

www.MainStreetMarketingBlog.com

Copyright 2014

Table of Contents

Idea One: Marketing Is Like A Nuclear Bomb

Marketing is like a nuclear bomb.

It's a game changer. Think about all the controversy you hear on the news about North Korea, Iran, and other nations with nuclear power.

Normally, countries like the US wouldn't care about a borderline third world country like Iran. Their army, navy, and airforce are simply not a legitimate threat. However, give 'em a nuclear weapon, and all of a sudden we're about to wet our pants we're so afraid.

I mean, really, think about it!

A wealthy, powerful nation like the United States is actually concerned (dare I say, scared) about what's going on in Iran because they *might* get a nuclear weapon. We spend more on our military than the rest of the world combined, yet we're afraid of some tiny third world country?

This is the power of nuclear weapons. They level the playing field between David and Goliath. They're an equalizer.

A nuclear bomb is like bringing a gun to a knife fight. Except, well, your gun can blow up the entire city.

Nuclear bombs are a game changer.

And marketing is like a nuclear bomb.

Marketing is THE magic bullet to a successful small business. It's the missing ingredient that will take you from good to great.

The power of marketing cannot be understated. A business can function with a variety of things going poorly. Marketing is not one of them. Without a predictable and steady flow of qualified leads, no business will survive. You simply cannot depend on "hustle" to keep the doors open. At least for long.

When you have a consistent flow of new customers coming in, you can afford to screw a lot of things up and still survive. The inverse is not true.

There's a reason good salespeople tend to be very, very well compensated. They are rainmakers. They bring in new customers.

A good marketing program accomplishes exactly that.

bottom of price wars.......*marketing* is the stone that will take down Goliath.

You'll understand that marketing is THE equalizer that allows locally owned, small businesses to thrive even when there is larger, well-funded competition out there.

You'll understand that your role as a business manager is working on, not in, your business.

You'll understand that marketing is a game-changer. When you refuse to play by someone else's rules of how a business "should be" operated, you've taken the first step in creating more profit in your business.

Which brings me to my next point....

If you have a marketing budget, you're a moron.

I'm not trying to be mean, but think about it for a second: marketing is supposed to make you money. It's NOT an expense. **It's an investment.**

Budgets are for expenses. Budgets are for things that *cost* you money.

Specifically, budgets are designed to keep us from spending too much money on something.

Many people have an entertainment budget. Why? Because you don't turn a profit by going to a movie or going to your favorite restaurant. It *costs* you money.

Most 10 year olds with a weekly allowance understand this, so why don't the vast majority of business owners get it?

Unless you're a Keynesian economist who thinks we need to spend money to get out of debt, this is pretty much common sense stuff!

Again, I will repeat: budgets are for expenses. Budgets are for things that *cost* you money. Budgets are for doing damage control on our expenses. Budgets are arbitrary limits on what we think we can afford to spend (notice I didn't use the word invest) on certain *expenses.*

In case we need a quick review, expenses are things like

- toilet paper
- gasoline
- printer ink

None of these are *directly related* to generating revenue. Now, of course, it would definitely be hard to close a big contract if you had a sore butt, your company car was low on gas, and the office printer was out of ink.

But these expenses do not inherently generate sales. They are means to an end.

Still with me? This isn't rocket science. Expenses cost you money; investments make you money.

Pretty simple, right?

If you've got a pen handy, underline the next sentence:

Marketing is not an expense; therefore, you should not have a "marketing budget."

"Budgeting" dollars for marketing is like budgeting how much money you want to make. Would you make a "budget" for your income goals? Hell no. You don't want to minimize or control how much money you make. You want to increase it. Hopefully exponentially!

If anything, your business should have a marketing *goal.* Not a budget. A *goal* of how much you hope to invest every year. Think about it: the more you can afford to invest in marketing, the healthier your business is. It's a reliable *indicator* of sustainable future profits. Every time your marketing system acquires a new customer, the present *and* future cash flow of your business increases.

If you're investing a lot in smart marketing, this means that your marketing is working.........which means your business is growing.

Marketing, if you're doing it right (which you should be by the time you finish this book), is a profit center. You spend $1, you get $2 back. Or $5. Or $10. Marketing is an investment. Not an expense.

It makes you money!

If I offered you $20 in exchange for your $10 bill, how many times would you make that trade? If you answered "As many times as I could," then you're right. Fortunately for you, most business owners are ignorant of how this works.

Saying you have a "marketing budget" is like saying, "Well, I like the trade we have going here. I give you $10, you give me $20. But let's cap it. I wouldn't want to profit *too much.*"

Similarly, many companies have a budget for marketing. To me, this makes no sense.

Now, I understand that when you're first starting out, you don't really know what a new customer's lifetime value is worth to you. You don't really know how many leads will come in as a result of your marketing. That's okay (we'll get to that later in the book).

The point here is to rid yourself of the outdated, ineffective, and downright stupid concept known as the "marketing budget."

Don't place arbitrary restrictions on your profits!

Do commit yourself to a renewed focus on marketing. It will change your business. And your life.

It's a leveler.

An equalizer.

A game changer.

Marketing is like a nuclear bomb.

Idea Two: Marketing Is Like Banking

Marketing is like banking, as much as I hate to say it.

I have a love/hate relationship with banks. They *are* usually the "cheapest" source of capital, but they're also more conservative than Ronald Reagan when it comes to lending out that capital.

Banks don't take unnecessary risks. They know their numbers, inside and out. If your debt/equity ratio isn't where they want it to be, well, guess what? Your loan request probably won't be approved.

Banking is math-driven. It's not a business for creative people who like to follow their heart, take risks, and other fluffy nonsense.

At its most basic level, banking is the business of arbitrage. It's buying low, selling high. Intuition may play a very small role in the process of lending out money, but that intuition is *always* backed by numbers that justify it.

Period.

With that in mind, you should think more like a bank! **Marketing should be numbers-driven.**

It's not about what you think is cute, creative, or cool. It's a numbers game.

Ad agencies and other "creative" businesses may think otherwise, but they have a financial incentive to feed you a line of bullshit. Their ads not working? Well, you simply need to buy more ads!

"Saturation is key," they say. What they *don't* tell you is they get a commission off of every media buy you make. They have no idea if what they're doing is working, and they profit off the fact that you don't, either.

If your unique selling proposition or competitive advantage is the ignorance of your customers (ad agencies, I'm talking to YOU), you need to rethink your business model......or someone else will.

Again, I repeat, marketing should be numbers-driven. In no other area of your business would you blindly spend money on something without at least making an attempt to track the results.

Why should marketing be any different?

If you cannot accurately measure the effectiveness of an advertisement, *you should immediately cancel that advertisement.*

(Usually the best way to measure your marketing is with online "landing pages." I'll explain more on that later)

You can't manage what you don't measure.

So, again, I repeat: you must *measure your marketing.*

The best way to do this is by using simple "landing pages," which I'll explain later in the book. For now, all you need to know is that a landing page is essentially the online equivalent of telling a potential customer to clip out your coupon and bring it in to the store to receive a special deal. If you count the number of redeemed coupons, you can accurately measure the effectiveness of a promotion.

This same process is easier (and more accurate) when you use online "landing pages" to measure everything for you. It's easy to set up, takes about five minutes.

Unfortunately, most small business owners do not measure anything. This puts them at an *extreme* disadvantage.

Alison Werder used to be one of these small business owners...but not anymore! Alison founded the *Ali J Boutique*, a retail women's clothing store.

While her business has had steady growth since its launch in 2011, Alison felt "something was missing" in her marketing.

That missing ingredient was *measurement.*

But it didn't take long for Alison to see the value of measuring her marketing...

Her very first campaign brought in 325 customers, all from a $100 Facebook ad!

The ad itself was surprisingly simple: Alison created a landing page using Frontdesk software, and then filmed a quick video inviting local ladies to check out her upcoming Fall Fashion Show (a live, in-store event).

She offered a coupon to anyone that signed up.

The results were spectacular—325 ladies signed up for the coupon, and almost overnight, Alison built a list of customers. The live event was attended by 150 ladies the next Friday evening, *and generated $7500 in sales.*

Oh, and did I mention The Ali J Boutique is located in a rural town of just 1200 people?

More important than the initial sales generated at the live event, Alison created an incredible asset for her business: a list of customers.

Would *your* business benefit from 325 new customers?

How about a live, in-store event that attracts 150 people?

This is the power of measurable marketing.

If you're selling used cars, your business won't last long without a sufficient number of "warm" buyers checking out your inventory. If you own a restaurant, you won't survive without a steady flow of hungry customers. If you're a realtor, you won't be in the business long if you sit on your butt and wait for people to call you.

Don't *wait* for people to buy. Be proactive and *sell* your products and services!

It all starts with creating measurable marketing campaigns. The keyword here is *measurable.*

Whatever the business, having a reliable marketing system in place that delivers customers to you will make things much easier. But we can't accomplish this without first knowing our numbers.

And that means we've got to measure!

Creating marketing systems that generate **a** predictable flow of inbound leads is the one thing that will change your business.

And your life.

Think about it: how awesome would life be if you could focus your time only on customers that are ready *and* eager to buy from you? This is the goal.

Unfortunately (or fortunately, depending on how you look at it), most business owners simply do not get this.

I've found that local business owners either don't have the time to do proper marketing, or they don't really understand it.....or both. Entrepreneurs and business managers tend to blindly toss dollars into marketing every month, not really knowing if what they're doing is working.

There's no measurement. No tracking. No accountability. I mean, seriously, *is there any part of your business that is as ignored as marketing*? Do you settle for mediocre customer service, product quality, or accounting accuracy? Of course not! Don't let marketing be the exception. It needs to be done right. Everything else depends on it!

Small businesses need to squeeze every last ounce of effectiveness out of their marketing dollars. Frankly, if you're a small business owner reading this, you work too damn hard to piss away money on ads that don't work.

You deserve better.

Improving your marketing begins with a fundamental shift in how you *think* about marketing.

Most business owners view marketing as a necessary evil. An expense. A black hole that sucks up money. A cost of doing business.

They are wrong.

To their credit, the masses *do* understand that if they quit marketing, their businesses probably wouldn't last long. So they blindly spend thousands of dollars on newspaper ads, radio campaigns, and a $5,000 fancy pants website that no one knows how to update or make changes to. Except the web designer....who happily bills $50/hour for website changes.

And what do they have to show for all of this? Not much.

I like asking business owners and managers a simple question: what part of your marketing is most effective right now? Many give a vague answer like, "Well, our print ads seems to be doing pretty well."

Huh?

They *seem* to be doing pretty well?

What the heck does that even mean?

If you are really *wowing* people with great customer service and an enjoyable buying experience, you will probably have a lot more than one future purchase and one referral! But, to be safe, it's a good idea to always be conservative.

Once we have a reasonably accurate calculation of a customer's LTV, *then* we can begin to formulate a marketing strategy. Using the car dealership example, we technically can afford to spend $1,500/month on radio ads to generate just one customer. Even then, we're still making $3,000 (this customer will buy again and refer a friend)!

While formulating this strategy, remember to factor in the *timing* of your cash flow.

While each new customer has an average LTV of $4,500, the immediate cash flow is only $1,500. So unless you have deep pockets *or* are in an aggressive growth phase, you probably can't afford to spend a lot more to acquire a customer than their initial purchase is worth. For example, if the initial purchase is worth $1,500 to you, try not to spend more than that per new customer.

Exceptions prove the rule.

That being said, realizing you can afford to invest more in customer acquisition is a HUGE, HUGE, HUGE competitive advantage.

Underline this next sentence: **the business that invests the most in marketing, wins.**

The key word here is "invest." Do *not* blindly throw money at marketing. That won't work. You can outspend your competition five to one buying stupid advertising that doesn't work, and they'll still dominate you if they have an effective, measurable marketing strategy.

Quality, not quantity.

Marketing is like banking, and bankers know their numbers.

Once you *know your numbers*, you will quickly realize you can probably afford to invest a lot more in customer acquisition than you currently are. Chances are, the competition is grossly underinvesting, too. This is a HUGE opportunity.

If the competition falsely believes they can only spend $500/month on radio ads, they might generate 5 quality leads a month from that. Once you realize that you can profitably invest at least $1,000 to acquire a new lead, it's a no-brainer to competition falsely believes….they cannot "justify" that expense.

If you're a car dealer, consider a gift-wrapped box containing a gift card to a nice restaurant 75 miles away, with a hand-written note saying, "Here's an excuse to take your new car on a little road trip. Enjoy!"

Oh, and throw in a $30 gas card so the experience doesn't cost them anything. *It's virtually guaranteed* they will tell their friends about this extra touch, and they'll be reassured that buying from *your* dealership was the right decision. These are the kind of customers that gladly refer friends.

Referrals do not happen because you did what was required, or simply met the customer's expectations. Enthusiastic referrals happen when you creatively *exceed* expectations.

Imagine how much you could increase your sales by designing a system that ensures every customer has this kind of experience….

Again, if you're a car dealer, including a "Thank You" gift package like this would probably cost less than $75. Once you begin to think in terms of lifetime value versus initial transaction, including this "wow" experience is a no-brainer!

Notice how this entire scenario is driven by an awareness of the numbers. Most business owners would immediately make a snap judgment that they can't "afford" to do something like that.

The truth is that you can't afford *not* to.

Like a banker, when you know your numbers, decision-making is pretty easy. Marketing is a numbers game.

It's profit-driven.

It's quantitative.

Marketing is like banking.

Idea Three: Marketing Is Like Farming

Marketing is like farming. It's a profit-driven process. Nobody farms "just for fun." Nobody farms hoping to break even. Nobody farms and knowingly loses money every year because "they enjoy it."

Farming is damn hard work.

Sure, some folks have a romantic, nostalgic attachment to the farming lifestyle, but they ultimately do it to make a living.

It's about profit.

Think about it: there's a reason the term "hobby farm" exists. It implies that every other farm is *not* a hobby. It's a business. And businesses exist to generate profit for their shareholders. In the case of most small businesses, that means: the owner and their family.

Farmers may love John Deere green and the smell of fresh cow crap at 5 AM, but they ultimately endure all of this for one thing: harvest.

As the late great Stephen Covey said, "Begin with the end in mind."

If you're a farmer, the "end" you're aiming for is harvest time. Harvest is payday, when you finally get to monetize what you've been working on all spring and summer.

I grew up in a community dominated by agriculture. If you weren't a farmer yourself, you probably knew someone who was. Well, you probably knew like twenty people who farmed. And if for some strange reason you didn't, you definitely knew people who indirectly worked in agriculture: livestock production, ag-related manufacturing, logistics, etc.

If you didn't personally (directly or indirectly) work in agriculture, your business was probably supported by all of the wealth generated by the regional farming community. Heck, even the public sector was and is dependent on tax revenues collected from the agriculture sector.

Such is life in the small town Midwest.

Which brings me back to our third big idea: marketing is like farming.

But first, some context:

Prehistoric man survived by hunting. Sociologists call this the "hunter-gatherer" age.

Before humans discovered agriculture, your survival depended on your ability to hunt and kill your next meal. If you weren't a skilled hunter, you would starve to death. This process repeated itself every day. *Every day* you needed to go out and hunt. You couldn't hunt in the spring and then wait until fall to go hunting again. It was a daily process. For prehistoric man, this was a brutal lifestyle.

If you wanted an evening meal, you needed to wake your ass up and earn it......every single day. Over and over and over again.

The discovery of agriculture changed all of this.

For the first time in human history, mankind was able to plan. Life took on more meaning than mere survival. For the first time, humans had a little bit of time leftover to explore meaningful topics like spirituality, art, and science. Not that farming was easy—but it sure beat hunting wooly mammoths and saber-toothed tigers...every single day.

With the discovery of agriculture, humans could now plant a given amount of seeds in the spring, and reasonably expect to harvest a given amount of food in the fall.

Survival was no longer a game.

For the first time, humans were masters of their own fate.

As it turns out, commerce has a lot to do with agriculture.

Unfortunately, most business owners are stuck in the hunter-gatherer mindset. They go out and struggle day in and day out to sell stuff. They can't take days off, or they won't be able to pay the bills.

Every day they have to wake up and sell, sell, sell.

For most owners of brick n mortar small businesses, their income is directly linked to the time they spend working. They are trading hours for dollars.

Usually we refer to this arrangement as a "job."

Is *that* what you signed up for?

Now, there's something admirable about this sort of hustle. The Protestant work ethic (combined with economic freedom) created the prosperity that has been the hallmark of Western civilization.

But.....

Wouldn't it be nice to make *more* money by working *less*?

You know, working smarter. Not harder.

It's time to reimagine your business. Instead of hunting for a living, I recommend that you strongly consider getting into the farming business.

Farming is all about "yield." And so is marketing.

Here's the thing: you can't harvest without planting seeds….and nurturing those seeds!

If farming was as easy as renting land, planting some seeds in the spring, then returning to harvest those seeds in the fall, well, everybody would do it!

Obviously, it's not that easy.

Farmers don't simply take a vacation from April to October. There's work to be done. If they want to harvest, they have to nurture the seeds they planted.

In a very literal sense, farmers plant thousands of little money trees every year. With a lot of hard work and a little luck, they will reap a harvest each fall.

Even amongst those of us who didn't grow up in farming communities, we understand that a lot of work takes place between the planting and harvesting stages of farming.

Marketing is like farming.

Your leads need to be nurtured. And it usually takes a long time! Harvest (selling stuff) is not synonymous with planting (generating leads).

And contrary to popular belief, placing an order for $1,000 worth of print advertising isn't "marketing." It's just planting.

The *real* work begins once your advertising generates a flood of leads that raise their hands and say, "Hey, I'm interested in what you have to sell."

Farmers earn the right to harvest by putting in the work from April-October.

Most businesses think they can skip all of this.

In doing so, they forego a *majority* of the sales they should be harvesting.

The key to transforming your business is getting really damn good at May, June, July, August, and September. Learn to develop prospects into paying customers.

Plant seeds; nurture the leads.

The real money to be made in most businesses is found in the "in-between." The "in-between" process of identifying a prospect and that prospect actually buying from you.

Most locally owned businesses depend on random luck to attract "ready to buy" customers. They foolishly ignore the majority of their leads that aren't ready to buy, *right now.* In doing so, they unknowingly flush large sums of money right down the toilet.

It's almost as if they're saying, "Oh, you're not ready to buy right now? Well screw you, don't waste our time."

This problem is magnified in industries with a lengthy sales cycle, such as real estate. Typically, someone thinking about buying or selling a house starts researching 6-12 months before making a decision. This means that at any moment in time, the vast majority of prospects are *not* ready to buy or sell. And this drives real estate agents crazy.

Except Debbie Caylor.

Debbie discovered the principles of *Main Street Marketing* in 2013. She knew she needed to start measuring her marketing (and building a list of prospects), but she wasn't sure what to "offer" prospects in her advertisements.

Unlike some businesses, she couldn't offer free samples or coupons. It's difficult to run a profitable marketing campaign if you give away free houses!

Debbie decided to offer something extremely valuable that would attract buyers and sellers to sign up on her landing pages...*a free book!*

Debbie authored a 200+ page book about her local real estate market, and gave it away for free. This was the perfect offer for a business with a lengthy sales cycle.

The free book appealed to anyone that was even thinking about buying a house! She generated *hundreds of new leads* (in an industry where most agents are lucky to have a dozen leads at any given time).

And best of all, writing the book positioned Debbie as the authority on local real estate. After all, she "wrote the book" on the local market!

Literally.

By building and cultivating a list of potential clients, *Debbie quadrupled her sales in the year following the publication of her book.*

This is the power of measurable marketing.

The difference between making just enough for payroll every week and making six figures is learning how to convert a high % of interested prospects into paying customers. After all, anyone can buy a bunch of ads and attract large numbers of prospects—it's knowing how to convert those prospects into actual sales that makes one rich.

The goal of effective marketing is to plant seeds and *develop leads.* Lucky for us, that rhymes….so don't forget it!

Marketing, in and of itself, rarely results in new customers coming to your business and purchasing right away (unless you're in a low cost, impulse-purchase business like fast food). At least 60% of the time, leads generated by good marketing must be nurtured *before* they buy your product or service.

Marketing is like farming.

Numerous studies have shown that 60% (or more) of customers will *not* buy the first time they come in contact with your product. **However, if these customers are followed up with and "nurtured" via a marketing funnel that educates them about your product and establishes trust, they *will* eventually buy.**

In other words, if you *don't* have an automated and systematic follow up system, you are missing out on 60% of the value of the leads generated by your advertising dollars.

If you strike up a conversation with a farmer and the first words out of your mouth are, "I think I can increase your yield by 60% or more," you will have his undivided attention!

Increasing your sales by 60% or more is the difference between retiring at 70 and retiring at 40. It's the difference between driving a used Pontiac and driving a brand new Cadillac. It's the difference between price shopping and ordering whatever you want to when you go out to eat.

Your life would be a lot different if your business's sales increased by 60%.

Would you like to increase *your* revenues by 60% or more? Design a marketing funnel that nurtures your leads!

Don't worry if the majority of these leads don't buy right away.

They might not buy within the week, month, or even year!

But when the following 3 conditions are met, your prospects *will* buy:

1. The prospect is **educated** about your product and its value
2. The prospect **trusts** you
3. The prospect is **ready** to buy

You have control over two out of the three. It's up to YOU to educate your prospects about the value of your offering, and why their life will be better once they purchase. It's up to YOU to earn their trust by positioning yourself as an expert.

What you do *not* have control over is when they're ready to buy.

Maybe they don't need your product for another 7 months, but they're doing some research. Maybe they just don't have the money right now, but they're saving up. Maybe they're convinced and ready to buy, but their spouse isn't so sure. Whatever the case, you really don't have control over this third condition.

Do everything you can to educate the prospect and earn their trust (we'll get into specific strategies later in the book). When they trust you and understand the value of your offering, they'll be ready to buy soon enough.

Would you feel sorry for a farmer that planted seeds in April, took an extended vacation to Europe, then returned in October to a meager harvest?

Probably not.

Farming is a process!

And so is marketing.

Most businesses have no follow-up system, whatsoever (many sales gurus call this process a "sales funnel").

These businesses are essentially saying, "We don't care about the 60% or more of prospects that will buy some day but don't buy right now. We don't care about them."

To be fair, it is generally a good idea to spend your time with people ready and eager to buy. Since time is our most valuable resource (you can always get a loan from the bank if you need *money*), it makes sense to spend it wisely.

This is why our follow up strategy needs to be a *system.* It cannot be random or spontaneous. If your conversion strategy depends on whether you "feel like" following up with prospects, it will fail. You must design a system that is protected from human error...aka laziness.

And a properly designed follow up *system* should be as automated as possible.

(Don't worry, software can do most of this for you)

The system nurtures the leads generated by your advertising, so you can spend your time working with customers at the end of the funnel: ready and eager to buy.

Let's say you own a retail store, and the LTV of every new customer is $350. You might attract 100 leads through a local newspaper ad, out of which only 10 buy something right away. That means you have 90 prospects that are interested in your product, but simply need to be properly educated on its value!

Do you see where I'm going with this?

Not all 90 will end up becoming paying customers. Maybe only 40 will. But by placing each lead into your follow up program, you are increasing the effectiveness of the ad from 10 sales to 50 (10 immediate purchases and 40 eventual purchases).....that's a 400% improvement!

Think back to chapter two. Marketing is like banking, so it's important to know your numbers. If each new paying customer has a $350 lifetime value, then an ad that generates 10 new purchases is worth about $3,500 to you.

However, if you have an effective follow up system that captures the other 90 leads, educates them, and over time builds trust with them, 40 of them *will eventually* buy. This means that your ad generated 50 sales! Fifty sales times a lifetime value of $350 per customer = $17,500.

Not bad.

So, in this example, the difference between a business with a follow up system and one without a follow up system...is $14,000!

If you only make money off of the ten customers that buy from you, you've made $3,500. If you develop all of your leads and get another 40 to eventually buy, you've made $17,500.

Again, the difference here is $14,000...and this is just from ONE AD.

In a car dealership, real estate office, or other high-dollar business, this paradigm shift can be worth literally *millions* of dollars to you!

You can't harvest what you don't plant...and nurture.

Marketing is about nurturing leads.

It's about staying in touch with leads.

It's about *automating a system* that stays in touch with leads.

It's about building trust with those leads.

It's about the May, June, July, August, and September that make the October harvest possible.

Marketing is like farming.

Idea Four: Marketing Is Like Warfare (what an ancient Chinese military strategist can teach us about outsmarting the competition)

Marketing is like warfare.

No really, it is. As much as we'd like to think that we're in some sort of *friendly* competition to make money, capitalism is anything but friendly. It's cutthroat. It's aggressive. It's Darwinian.

Only the strong survive.

While you might be casual friends with the competition, the truth is that they'd love nothing more than to put you out of business. If this were real war, I might use an adjective like "violent" to describe the competitive process. Your competition wants to stab you in the throat, cut off your head, and parade your body through the streets.

Internalize that mental image.

It *is* true that capitalism is not a zero-sum game. The pie grows bigger every year (even extreme liberals on fringe networks like MSNBC will quietly acknowledge this). That's why government redistribution schemes always backfire.

That being said, there is one element of capitalism that is *absolutely* a zero-sum game: direct competition.

Either your competition makes the sale or you do.

Either they get the customer or you do.

Every ideal prospect that chooses to buy from the bad guys is a sale you lost.

This isn't youth soccer; not everyone gets a trophy.

When you look at things from a competitive perspective, there is definitely a winner and a loser. Macroeconomics aside, capitalism IS a zero-sum game when viewed from a competitive standpoint.

And nice guys finish last.

You know that friendly guy who always shakes your hand at the weekly Chamber of Commerce meetings? Yeah, you know exactly who I'm talking about. Even though he works for the competition, he makes a point to always ask you about "how business is doing."

He might play nice at social gatherings, but this dude would love to see you go bankrupt. He'd love to watch your kids cry while the bank seizes your home. He would swoop in like a vulture and steal your wife if he could get away with it. He wants nothing less than total domination of the market.

And so do you, I hope.

It takes a sort of warrior mentality to succeed in the business world. "Mamby pamby" doesn't work as a management style. Marketing is a lot like warfare.

And as small business owners, we can learn a thing or two from studying military strategy.

When Ronald Reagan was asked his strategy on the Cold War, his reply was simple: "We win; they lose."

To achieve victory, we need to begin with the end in mind. Start with STRATEGY.

How will we get where we're going?

Sun Tzu made this a foundational principle in his famous treatise on military strategy, *The Art of War.*

"All men can see these tactics whereby I conquer, but what none can see is the strategy out of which victory is evolved."

Here's the takeaway: tactics are irrelevant. The specific

tactics you use to win the battle are *determined by the strategy*. There's a tool for every job. Screwdrivers can be wonderfully useful, but if you need to pound a nail into something, you better have a hammer. Likewise, a nuclear bomb is a terrific (and horrific) weapon; however, it is NOT more "effective" than a well-trained team of Navy SEALS.

Effectiveness is a dependent variable.

Effectiveness depends on the objective. What are you trying to accomplish?

When President Obama received intel that Osama Bin Laden was hiding out in Pakistan, did we drop a nuclear bomb on the compound?

Of course not.

Would it have killed him? Yes.

Would it have been the most efficient way of accomplishing the objective? No.

The strategy determined the tactic. The Navy SEALS were sent in. We won; they lost.

Score one for the good guys.

In the world of small business marketing, strategy is actually a competitive advantage. Why? Well, the answer is pretty simple: most small business owners HAVE NO STRATEGY.

They show up to work every day with the vague goal of "making more money."

There is no intentional plan.

If you even *have* a strategy, you're already ahead of the mediocre majority.

Let's assume for a moment you own a movie theater in a small town of 10,000 people. There is a city twenty miles away that has 50,000 people...and a large multiscreen cinema.

They are your competition.

You've determined that much of their business comes from *your* potential customers driving twenty miles out of the way to spend their money. You are losing out on tens of thousands of dollars a year in business, if not more. *This is a zero sum game.*

There will be a winner and a loser. Which one do you want to be?

If it were me, I'd do some research on the customers that are currently patronizing my movie theater:

- How old are they?
- How much money do they make?
- What kind of cars do they drive? (Hint: figuring this out is as simple as taking a quick stroll

through your parking lot)

- What genre of movies do they prefer?

This information will give us a basic understanding of our "ideal customer." The goal here is to identify the perfect customer so that we can create a marketing STRATEGY that is intentionally designed to attract more of THOSE KINDS OF CUSTOMERS.

We *don't* want to run general, vague ads that appeal to everyone. We want to identify our target market with a laser-like precision, and then draft a strategy aimed at getting more of THOSE KINDS OF CUSTOMERS. And yes, that means our marketing will intentionally exclude a lot of people.

Not all customers are created equal.

If you do some basic recon, you'll probably find that some customers spend more than others do. You'll find that some customers *always* buy a large popcorn and pop. You'll find that some customers go to movies three times a month. Maybe four.

Guess what?

THIS is the segment of customers you want to target. Have them fill out short surveys so you can find out more about them. Bribe them, if necessary. Very few people will turn down a free movie ticket or large popcorn in exchange for their mailing address and answering a few basic questions.

This information is GOLD to you. Once you identify a profile of your ideal client, you can focus all of your marketing dollars on targeting THEM, and *only* THEM.

Remember, we *could have* nuked Bin Laden's compound in Pakistan. It would have taken him out, but it would have been inefficient. It would have been a waste (of dollars *and* human life). Instead, we sent in a team of Navy SEALS. We identified our target market, and chose our tactics based on that.

The key point here is to recognize that a nuclear bomb *would* have worked. That would have been the easy way.

And the dumb way.

Most small business owners, almost by default, opt for this sloppy approach to marketing. Most don't know any better. They don't understand the idea of target marketing. They don't understand the role strategy plays in creating profits. They don't understand that the strategy should inform the tactics.

Marketing is like warfare! On the battlefield, there's a

winner and a loser. The only field where everyone gets a trophy is the cemetery.

To increase your chances of winning, realize that the wrong strategy executed perfectly will not help you.

Let's continue with the example of a small town movie theater...

After doing some research, we conclude that our best customers are those who appear to be making more than $100,000 a year, and are over 40 years old. When we walked the parking lot, we found a lot of BMW's and Cadillacs. Our surveys confirmed this qualitative observation. Armed with this new knowledge, we can now craft a STRATEGY aimed at acquiring more of *these* customers.

Our strategy is simple: by providing luxurious "extras" to our guests, we will be THE movie theater for local affluent moviegoers. Yes, experiencing a movie at our theater might be more expensive, but that's okay!

We've identified our ideal client as someone who is willing to pay for luxury. Our strategy revolves around dominating this market niche.

We will *not* be all things to all people. Our marketing budget will reflect this.

Remember, not all customers are created equal. Some customers are more profitable than others. In the case of a movie theater, some people will try to sneak in their own pop and candy. You really can't do anything about it, EXCEPT designing your marketing from the get-go to bring in customers that won't do this.

Again, not all customers are created equal. My apologies to Abe Lincoln, but it's true.

One of the first things I would do is set up some sort of joint venture with local luxury car dealerships. I'd approach the local Lexus dealer, Cadillac, BMW, etc. Offer them free movie passes they can give to their customers as a "thank you" for buying a car, or just taking a test drive.

(This would work with high end restaurants, jewelry stores, financial advisors, etc...any business who shares your ideal client but isn't direct competition)

This situation is a win-win: the dealership strengthens the bond with their customers by providing unexpected value, and you acquire new customers that perfectly fit your ideal customer profile. The movie tickets really don't cost you anything, as you make your profits on sales of concessions. This is a cheap and easy way to build your database of customers.

It's a no brainer.

Focus your marketing to appeal ONLY to your ideal customers.

We don't want any collateral damage of marketing dollars.

Pick your battles.

When you own a small business, waste is the enemy. We cannot afford to waste marketing dollars chasing prospects that are anything less than our ideal customer.

I think Sun Tzu would have been a rockstar small business owner. This guy knew a thing or two about strategy! Hundreds of years ago, an army could not simply win a battle by dropping a bomb, launching some missiles, or sending in drones. Warfare was an intricate game of chess. It was cat and mouse.

Sun Tzu realized the importance of having an intentional strategy, and basing tactics off of that strategy. *The Art of War* is FULL of references to the importance of strategy:

> "Strategy without tactics is the slowest route to victory. Tactics without strategy is the noise before defeat."

Translated into "practical" marketing advice, we want to design a program that increases our conversion ratio.

Think about it like this: **if all you do is increase your conversion ratio, you will create more profits without having to spend any money on additional advertising.**

You are taking advantage of the opportunities you already have. Sun Tzu would be all over this!

We want our tactics to not only be effective, but *efficient.*

If business A and business B both bring in 25 new customers with separate advertising campaigns, which one was better? We can't really know unless we figure out how much they spent to acquire those prospects, and what percentage of those prospects actually became paying customers.

Is your business measuring this? You should be.

And remember, efficiency is *not* the same thing as effectiveness. Snipers don't use shotguns.

Once we've established a strategy for *how* we're going to win, we can begin formulating the specific tactics to execute the strategy.

In a nutshell, what we're trying to do here **is focus our firepower on prospects that are predisposed to doing business with us.** Minimize the collateral damage of wasted advertising dollars.

Let's continue with the movie theater scenario.

Because we've done our research, we know that our cinema appeals to middle aged men in their peak earning years, many of which are driving luxury automobiles. Sure, there are plenty of other demographics that buy tickets, but folks who fit this description are our *ideal* clients. They are predisposed to wanting what we offer. To them, price is irrelevant. Every marketing dollar targeted at this demographic will produce exponentially higher ROI than blindly buying advertising that appeals to the general public.

Remember, we probably *would* reach some of these prospects by purchasing a general newspaper ad, but we could be more effective and efficient by targeting our marketing.

A nuclear bomb would not make Osama Bin Laden any more dead than a 5.56mm bullet fired from the rifle of a Navy SEAL.

Just because a tactic is effective does not mean it is efficient.

If the aforementioned movie theater hired me to do some marketing consulting, one of the first things I would do (following the identification of our ideal customer profile) is draft a direct mail campaign targeted at acquiring these "perfect" clients.

Studies have proven again and again that there is a direct correlation between the age of a customer and their trust of anything in "print." Members of the millennial generation don't draw this distinction. They view digital communication like texting, email, and social media as "legitimate."

Older customers do not.

To them, if something is in print, it is more credible and trustworthy (be it a newspaper ad, direct mail, or an actual book).

With this in mind, I would create a multi step direct mail campaign. I'd contact a list broker and obtain a list of customers that fit my target demographic:

- Males over age 45
- Making a six figure income
- Own a luxury car

I'd write a multiple page "sales" letter that speaks directly to them. It might sound something like this:

As we all know, there is no easy way to the top. If being successful were easy, everyone would do it. Those that have achieved financial freedom in life have paid a price to do so. It's hard work. It's stressful. That's why I want to offer you a FREE movie ticket to my cinema. I know you're a hard worker. I know that you could use an "escape" from responsibility. Even if it's only 120 minutes......

I'd bet large sums of money a marketing campaign like this would achieve an ROI so spectacular, most small business owners would think it's too good to be true.

That being said, this isn't rocket science.

By choosing my tactics *after* I've developed a strategy, I put myself in a situation with a high probability of success. We want to first identify prospects that are predisposed to wanting what we have, and then craft our marketing message to *specifically* appeal to them.

Put yourself in situations with a high probability of success. Fight battles you can win.

It follows that you are more likely to succeed when focusing your marketing efforts on your target market. Exclude everyone else.

Pick your battles.

Yes, we *want to* exclude the vast majority of potential customers. I'd rather have 2 customers come in that fit my ideal customer profile than 10 random prospects who do not.

Not all customers are created equal!

Some are more profitable than others.

In *The Art of War*, Sun Tzu repeated over and over again that most battles were won (or lost) before they were fought. The smart warrior chooses to fight battles they know they can win. The smart marketer does the same thing.

"He who knows which battle he should engage in and which he should avoid, will win."

"The winner, after careful preparation, is confident he will win the war before he wages battle. The losers, without preparation, engage the enemy first, merely *hoping* they will win the fight."

Let's say the movie theater in the bigger city can afford brand new digital projection technology, huge screens, and always gets the "first run" movies on opening weekend. Being the owner of a small town theater, you simply can't compete.

Or can you?

Again, you must pick battles you know you can win. Having the most resources is *not* the only relevant variable. Identify the variables you can compete and win on.

Can you offer lower prices?

Higher prices?

Can you offer a prepaid monthly membership?

Can your theater be an active member of the community by sponsoring events and visibly donating to charities?

Does your cinema have a personal newsletter that goes out to your customers every month?

Can you boost revenues by renting out your auditoriums to churches, business meetings, or other groups looking for a place to hold a meeting?

Can you offer a complimentary on-site babysitting service so parents with young children can enjoy a date night (without having to pay someone $20 to watch their kids)?

What can you be better at than the competition?

It doesn't matter if you're positioning your business on the low end or high end, *there is always a niche you can dominate.*

Imagine for a moment that you hardly have enough money to pay the bills. You cannot simply buy your way to success (this is the predicament of most small business owners).

To effectively fight the big boys, small businesses must play by a different set of rules. When you have fewer resources than your opponents, you must use unconventional tactics. Necessity really *is* the mother of invention when it comes to running a small business.

The answer to big budget traditional advertising is not to fight fire with fire.

Rather than trying to *outspend* the competition, small businesses need to *outthink* them.

Strategy before tactics! Any general could win a battle with enough soldiers to sacrifice. In fact, General Ambrose Burnside tried to do exactly that in 1862 at the infamous Battle of Fredericksburg.

Knowing he had tens of thousands of men to sacrifice (and the industrial machine of the Northern economy), General Burnside thoughtlessly ordered thousands of young men to their deaths in a futile attempt to take a heavily defended Confederate hilltop position.

Burnside carelessly assumed that with thousands of men at his disposal, eventually he would take the hill.

He was wrong.

Positioned behind a solid stonewall atop the hill, Confederate soldiers easily repelled each attack, completely devastating entire regiments of Burnside's men.

It was a slaughter, and President Abraham Lincoln soon relieved General Burnside of his command.

In marketing as in war, quality matters more than quantity! A surplus of resources is no substitute for strategy.

Being outnumbered forces you to leverage your creativity (General Robert E. Lee proved this at the Battle of Chancellorsville, where he defeated a Union Army *twice the size* of his forces. To this day, Lee's brilliant tactics at the Battle of Chancellorsville are studied in military academies).

Efficient and effective small business marketing requires the entrepreneurial equivalent of guerilla warfare.

Guerilla tactics work because they leverage strengths and avoid weaknesses.

Throughout history, "underdogs" have understood this concept out of necessity.

The Vietcong didn't fight in open fields; they wisely chose to engage the enemy only when they had an advantage.

They fought on their own terms.

Just because the enemy wants to fight in the open field doesn't mean you have to! The bad guys want you to fight on *their* terms. Make them fight on *yours.*

Think about David and Goliath: David won the battle because he refused to fight Goliath on his own terms! David leveled the playing field by changing how the battle was fought. Rather than trying to overcome his weakness, *he leveraged his strengths.* David chose to not wear heavy armor, and instead opted for a lighter, more agile weapon: a slingshot. By refusing to fight Goliath the traditional way, David won the battle (and cut off Goliath's head, for good measure).

According to political scientist Ivan Arreguín-Tof, using unconventional tactics is the key to success when you find yourself outnumbered and outgunned.

In a comprehensive academic study encompassing every major battle fought in the past 200 years, Arreguín-Tof found that the "Goliaths" of the world beat their lesser opponents roughly 70% of the time.

Think of this from the perspective of David—even when the underdogs foolishly chose to fight conventionally, they *still* managed to win nearly a third of the battles!

However, when the little guys decided to *change the rules of the game*—fight unconventionally—they actually won nearly 64% of the time.

The lesson is obvious: don't play to your opponent's strengths; make them react to *yours*.

Bigger isn't always better. Size is only one variable in a battle.

Identify your business's strengths, and choose a battle where *those* variables matter.

As Sun Tzu taught us, warfare is based on strategy. There are more factors than size or strength.

If this were not true……..

- American colonists would never have beaten the British.
- Texas freedom fighters would never have beaten the Mexican army.
- The Vietcong would never have forced American forces to retreat.
- The Soviets and/or Americans would have *crushed* the Taliban.

Small business marketing is no different: by refusing to play by your opponent's rules, you can drastically change outcomes. Just because most businesses blindly throw advertising dollars into billboards, print ads, and other traditional mediums *doesn't mean you have to!*

Having a smaller budget is often times a blessing, because it forces you to be more efficient with what you have.

Creativity can be a competitive edge.

According to 19th century Italian economist Vilfredo Pareto, 80% of outputs are produced by a mere 20% of inputs. This has huge implications for a small business's marketing strategy!

Rather than a "well-diversified" advertising portfolio, locally owned businesses should have a *laser-like focus* when it comes to marketing. Find out what marketing initiatives produce 80% of new revenue, and focus on leveraging these inputs! Furthermore, find out what demographic of customers produces 80% of the revenue, and market exclusively to them! The important word here is *efficiency.*

Small businesses don't have money to waste. We must do more with less.

Know the battlefield inside out. Study every variable,

and then exploit the ones that are in your favor.

Never fight a battle where your chance of victory is less than 80%.

Marketing is like warfare.

Know your strategy, and pick your battles.

Idea Five: Marketing Is Like Dating, Part One (And How To Use Landing Pages To Measure Your Marketing)

Imagine for a moment that you're seventeen years old.

You're a junior in high school. Even though you play on the football team, you're definitely not one of the "cool kids." On the social ladder of popularity, you're somewhere in the middle. Not a nerd, but not the varsity quarterback, either.

Your grades are pretty good, somewhere around a B average. Not *too* good where you'd be considered a geek, but good enough to get you into college.

You're playing it safe, right in the sweet spot of acceptance.

When you walk the halls in between classes, some people might recognize your face, but they probably don't know your name. You blend in pretty well. Your best friend told you that on a scale of 1-10, you're a solid "6."

Nothing to brag about, but hey……it could be worse.

All year you've been eyeing the girl who sits across from you in math class. Two desks to the left, to be exact.

Her name is Katie.

She has long, blonde hair, and an intellect that destroys the stereotype associated with it. Katie is the smartest girl in the class. And she's a cheerleader, too. The complete package.

Way out of your league.

You met her during orientation on the first day of freshman year. Ever since that fateful morning, you've told yourself you would work up the courage to ask her to prom. For some reason, it's still a possibility: she doesn't have a boyfriend, and no guy has asked her. Yet.

Time is ticking.

Katie's one of those girls that has it all. She's smart, sexy, and has a fun personality. Well, you *assume* she has a fun personality. You've never actually talked to her.

Marketing is like dating.

How often do you reach out to your prospects with solid offers? Most small business owners are content to place an ad in the newspaper that has their logo and contact information. They're not really making an offer, they're just letting people know they exist.

When all you do is advertise your logo, store hours, and contact information, you put all of the pressure on your prospect to take the initiative.

Bad idea.

Oh, and while we're on the subject, saying something idiotic like "Come on in for 10% off" is about the stupidest message you could pay to advertise. Unless you're selling a high priced item like automobiles or real estate, no one gives a shit about 10% off.

Seriously. It's almost insulting.

If a customer isn't already interested in what you're selling, a paltry offer like 10% off isn't going to convince them to give you a try. All you're accomplishing is the erosion of your profit margin on customers *who would have happily paid full price.* To make matters worse, you compromise your price integrity.

When the best promotion you can think of is "10% off," it sends a very clear message to all potential customers: wait until it goes on sale.

Okay, sorry about the angry rant. Back to the dating metaphor.

Most of the advertising I see produced by small businesses can be grouped into five categories:

1. *Blank stare*
2. "Hello, I exist."
3. "You going to prom this year?"
4. "If you want to go to prom with me, let me know."
5. "Katie, will you go to prom with me?"

As you can see, the manner in which the offer is worded changes everything. The meaning is *completely different* depending on how you construct the question.

While the following sounds like common sense, it might just change how you think about marketing.

Underline the idea I'm about to share with you. Get it tattooed on your forearm. Grab a scissors and cut this page out of the book, then frame it on your desk. It's that important.

Paradigm shift in 3, 2, 1…….okay, okay, here's the big idea:

The questions you ask determine the responses you get.

Pretty simple, right?

Easy enough. But here's the thing: 99% of small business

owners never think about their advertising this way. They think it's as easy as, "Buy ad; get results."

Yeah, not so much.

Let's analyze the 5 different types of questions you can ask in your advertising.

1. *The Blank Stare*

The "blank stare" isn't as much a form of advertising as it is *the absence* of advertising.

The blank stare approach is synonymous with the "build it and they will come" mentality. In my not-so-humble opinion, businesses that believe in this nonsense are either really arrogant or really stupid. Maybe both.

When you make absolutely zero effort to reach out to potential customers, don't be surprised when they make absolutely zero effort to reach out to *you*!

There's a classic advertising axiom that sums this up nicely: "Something happens when you don't advertise. Nothing."

Think back to the high school metaphor. What are the odds that Katie will end up going to prom with you if you never even attempt to reach out to her? Are you so conceited (possibly delusional) that you actually believe she will ask *you* to the prom?

Sitting there in math class day after day awkwardly staring at Katie will not make things any better. You have to market yourself.

Do *something.*

I often have small business owners tell me, "We're actually doing quite well, and we don't spend a dime on advertising. It's all word of mouth."

Congratulations, you're an idiot.

Think about it like this: how much is it costing you to *not* invest in marketing?

If your product or service is so valuable that you're doing "well" solely on word of mouth, imagine how much money you'd make if you proactively marketed your business!

When viewed from the perspective of *opportunity cost,* you are missing out on tens of thousands of dollars every year by stubbornly deciding that you don't need to do any marketing.

I view this mentality with the same contempt as I would some jackass high school athlete who thinks he's so good looking that the ladies will simply approach *him* when prom season approaches.

Like I said, the "blank stare" approach is either ignorant or arrogant. In all likelihood, both.

Don't just stare at Katie. That's weird.

You're better than that.

2. "Hello, I exist."

This category of messaging is slightly better than the "blank stare" idiocy mentioned earlier. Slightly better.

Which isn't saying much.

This category is where 80% of small business owners are stuck. They buy a token newspaper ad with an uninteresting picture, the name of their business, their store hours, and some basic contact information.

Oh, and usually there's a cheesy tagline somewhere in there.

The *Hello, I exist* advertisement promises no value to the customer; it offers no compelling reason to respond. It simply says, "Here we are."

Sure, it's *implied* that they want you to stop in and buy stuff, but there is no offer being made. At best, you're reminding people that you exist.

If you're a locally owned pizzeria, an ad like this is not going to generate a flood of new customers that want your pizza. Unless someone was already planning on going out for pizza that night, seeing a *Hello, I exist* advertisement will not move people to take action.

If your ads look like this, you might as well flush your money down the toilet. Maybe someone will find those soggy dollars and actually put them to good use.

This is the equivalent of passing Katie in the hall, smiling, and saying "Hi."

I suppose it's progress if you've never said a word to her. If she didn't know you existed, well, now she does.

Baby steps.

But if the goal is to convince Katie that you're worthy enough to take her to prom, reminding her you exist is *not* going to get the job done.

You're showing up with a knife to a gunfight.

Again, this is better than no communication at all, but think about it from the perspective of Katie: she has no idea of your intentions. She has no idea you desperately want her to go to prom with you.

Best-case scenario is she smiles and thinks to herself, "He is friendly."

The difference between a fuzzy feeling and an actual response is the difference between zero and one. It's infinite.

If your "prospect" has no idea of the value you are offering, because you're not offering anything but your damn contact information and store hours, what in the hell makes you think they will take you up on your offer?

Well, lack thereof.

Customers cannot respond to an offer that does not exist.

3. "You Going To Prom This Year?"

This type of question is considered by many sales experts to be a "qualifying" question.

Now, this isn't the *dumbest* thing you could say. It's much better than the *blank stare* or *I exist* approaches. But it's still not perfect.

Don't get me wrong; I have nothing against qualifying your prospects. It's an important part of the sales process.

Anyone who's been in sales more than a few days understands that if you want to make good money, you can't waste your time with prospects that are kicking tires.

Time is your most valuable resource as a salesperson, so you can't afford to invest it in people who aren't ready to buy.

Here's the catch....

Your prospects shouldn't realize you are "qualifying" them. The questions you ask should be indirect. There's nothing more annoying to a customer than realizing the salesperson views them as a statistic, and is trying to "qualify" them.

From the customer's perspective, traditional qualifying questions come off as, "I'm trying to figure out if you are worth my time."

Think of the typical first date. Would you ask questions like:

"So, how much money do you make?"

"Are you a Christian?"

"Did you vote for Obama?"

"Are you a virgin?"

Now, you might be silently wondering about these topics. The answers to these questions might be a litmus test for potential mates. Maybe it's non-negotiable that you want to marry someone who graduated from college and has a professional career. Maybe you refuse to marry a conservative Republican. Whatever your motivations, I hope you would not open up your first date with a string of questions like this.

You shouldn't do this with your advertising, either.

Marketing is like dating.

If you're "qualifying" your customer, they shouldn't realize it. Instead of directly asking the questions you are wondering about, weave them into a casual conversation.

If the ultimate goal is taking Katie to prom, first strike up a conversation with her. Even a comment about the weather is okay—just get a dialogue started. Anything will do. Eventually, you can weave in some stealthy "qualifying" questions.

"So, Katie, seen any good movies lately?" (trying to figure out if she has a boyfriend)

"Did you go to prom last year?" (indirectly bringing up the topic in a nonthreatening way)

Once the ice is broken in a conversation, you can be a little more blunt. People hate to be sold, but they love to buy.

It's all about planting seeds and getting the customer to *know*, *like*, and *trust* you.

Once you've developed a casual relationship with a customer, they won't mind if you ask a qualifying question that's a little more direct.

Customers actually welcome it!

They wouldn't be talking to you if they weren't at least *interested* in what you had to offer.

By intentionally building trust *before* you make any type of offer, you earn the right to make the offer. At the very least, ask a direct qualifying question.

Say something like, "So Katie, you think you'll go to prom this year?"

This is sneaky. If Katie really *doesn't* want to go to prom, she'll say so! If she is planning on going to prom and has already been asked by another guy, she'll say so. If she plans on going to prom but is still "available," she will probably hint at it without saying it outright:

"Yeah, I'd like to. Do you think you'll end up going?"

In all likelihood, she would have preferred to just say, "Yes," or "Yeah I'd like to."

Fortunately for you, once a legitimate back and forth conversation has been started, it's awkward to stop. As much as they'd like to, most people will not give you a one-word reply.

If they *do*, that's an indicator they're probably not "qualified." At least not right now.

The worst-case scenario is getting indirect confirmation that a prospect isn't ready to buy. Either way, you win.

That little extra sentence, "Do you think you'll end up going," makes all the difference in the world. Whether or not Katie wants to continue the conversation with us is irrelevant. **She has given us permission to!** In fact, to avoid an awkward one-word response, she's asked *us* a question!

The tables have been turned.

Think of this as marketing ju-jitsu. We are using the energy from our "opponent" to move us closer to our goal.

Now that we have Katie's permission to state our intentions, it's time to make an offer.

4. "If you want to go to prom with me, let me know."

This is the coward's way out. Offers wrapped in this packaging are the difference between six figures and making just enough money to pay for your bills every month.

The "Let Me Know" offer is only slightly better than the "I exist" offer. Why? Well, for starters, you are giving the customer permission to say, "Okay, just looking."

This is a sales killer.

Most retails stores can exponentially increase their profits simply by training their sales team to ask, "Hi, I'm Tim. What advertisement brought you in today?"

Notice that this question cannot be answered with a one-word response.

In fact, it demands some type of explanation. It would be awkward for the customer to say, "No thanks, just looking."

And if they *do* say that, you can be pretty sure they're not serious buyers anyways.

The "Let Me Know" is a form of retreat. It's surrender.

It's essentially saying, "I'm not really a sales person. I'm too scared to sell. I don't want to offend anybody. If you're ready to buy right now, I can help ring you up. Otherwise, don't mind me."

If this is you, realize that you are *not* a salesperson. You are a cashier.

There is a difference.

This is the approach of most small business owners. I hate to break it to you, but if this is you, *a machine could do your job.*

If you don't want to "pester" customers by diagnosing their true needs, and finding solutions that will solve their problems, why not just install a self-checkout at your business? What's the point of paying a sales team?

Most people will attempt to justify this nonsense with, "People don't like being on the receiving end of a hardsell. I don't want to make them feel uncomfortable." This is bullshit.

And a total straw man argument.

I'm *not* advocating giving someone a hardsell to try and convince them to buy something they really don't want or need.

And, really, it makes you look like an idiot if the best you can come up with is, "Katie, well, ummmm, if you want to go to prom with me, well, let me know."

Want to know what Katie is thinking when you ask her something like that?

"This guy is a loser. He doesn't have the decency to properly ask me out; he indirectly asked *me* to ask him."

Once you've earned the customer's trust, don't be shy!

Imagine for a moment you're at a friend's house. Your buddy casually mentions to you, "If you want some chips, help yourself. They're in the kitchen."

How likely would you be to get off your ass, walk into the kitchen, and get some chips? It requires *effort* on your part.

It requires *you* to take initiative.

Compare this to a similar, yet profoundly different offer: your friend walks up to you while you're still sitting on the couch, and offers you a plate of chips.

All you have to do is reach out and accept the direct offer.

While these two offers are similar, they are presented in entirely different ways.

Realize that as a culture, we frown upon taking the initiative when other people are involved.

Even when someone says "Make yourself at home, help yourself to whatever you want," *most of us won't do it.*

But if someone walks up to us with a fresh plate of cookies, we'll take one!

Why? Because if someone makes you a direct offer of value, it's almost rude *not* to accept. The tables have been turned.

Now, this doesn't mean you can say, "Bill, would you like to buy a car today?" and expect people to just say "yes" to avoid embarrassment.

It *does* mean you can offer people valuable information and obtain permission to build a relationship.

If I owned a used car lot, instead of simply asking every customer for their contact information, I would reposition the offer so it creates value for the customer:

"Tom, I wrote a free 11-page report on how to make sure you're getting the best deal possible on a used car. It includes some tips and tricks I've learned over the years on how to negotiate with dealers and get the best value for your dollar. Would you like me to mail it to you?"

This is PROFOUNDLY DIFFERENT from the way most car dealers operate. Most car dealers simply say, "Hey Tom, fill out this form so we can get your contact information."

There is no exchange of value here. The customer is giving something up and not getting anything in return.

No wonder most people don't want to give up their contact information.

It's the business equivalent of being raped. There is no

value for value exchange. There is no mutual benefit. It's one-sided.

By repositioning the offer, we completely change how the customer views the act of "giving up" their contact info.

Customers are not stupid. They know that when a business collects their information, they will probably be flooded with endless promotional junk mail. However, if we give them a *reason* to exchange their contact information, they will be glad to do so.

By repositioning the request for contact information in such a way, most small businesses can build their customer database 40% faster.

Or more.

Always, always, always be proactive in your marketing. Take the initiative. Make an *irresistible* offer to potential customers that *demands* a response.

Leave nothing to chance.

5. "Katie, will you go to prom with me?"

Level five. This is the sweet spot. If you want to

transform your business with a flood of new customers, make sure all of your advertising fits this description.

The key here is to always make a *direct* offer. None of this indirect, "Let me know" nonsense. Make a *direct* offer.

Before school, drive to the flower shop. Get a bouquet of roses. Surprise Katie and pop the question!

"Katie, will you go to prom with me?"

If you've nurtured a relationship with her to the point that she doesn't view you as a complete stranger, there is a good chance she will accept your offer. Katie knows, likes, and trusts you. You're not viewed as just another guy. You're not viewed as just another salesman.

And now you have a date to the prom!

Notice that this is a firm, specific question. You are not hedging your bets. Not one bit. You're putting yourself out there, *fully accepting the possibility that she might reject you.* You are extending a direct, specific offer.

This is hugely important in marketing.

All marketing campaigns should have a specific, measurable outcome. Every ad you run needs to try and convince prospects to take a *specific* action. Don't leave it up to them to decide what to do.

Tell them what you want them to do!

It can be downloading a free PDF report, signing up for your monthly newsletter, stopping in for half off drinks at happy hour, whatever. The point is that each time you spend money on advertising, *there needs to be a specific call to action that can be measured.*

For example, your ad can drive prospects to a special website with a landing page that asks them for their email address. This way, you can count exactly how many people took you up on your offer. Most of the ads I read in the newspaper or hear on the radio make no such offer. They simply say, "Come on in to our restaurant. The food is good."

How in the hell are you supposed to measure if an ad like that is working?

Most small businesses dodge the question, and say something like, "Well, I can definitely tell there's a decrease in customers when we stop advertising."

Really?

How much of a decrease?

Enough to justify the expense of designing and running the ad? Furthermore, if you cannot accurately measure the effectiveness of an ad, there's no way to tweak it. Maybe you can change the headline, change the size of the ad, add some color, etc. If there's no way to QUANTITATIVELY measure the effectiveness of an ad, how will you ever know?

You cannot manage what you cannot measure, so get used to making direct offers. I guarantee that it will transform your business.

The easiest way to make direct offers (so that you can measure your marketing) is by using *landing pages* in your marketing.

A landing page is a simple one-page website that has one purpose, and one purpose only: *collect the contact information of your customer.*

Usually a landing page will ask for the customer's name and email in exchange for downloading a free report, coupon, exclusive video, or some other valuable offer. If the customer isn't willing to sign up, they won't get the "prize."

Fair enough, right?

Good landing pages are clean looking, simple, and have nothing else on the page EXCEPT a place for the customer to enter their contact information.

The less confusion, the better.

You want to force the customer to *make a decision.*

Either they give you their information, or they leave the page. There is no in between.

Because of the binary nature of a landing page (either you get their contact info or you don't), there is no room for ambiguous metrics like page views, clicks, bounce rate, time on page, etc.

The only thing that matters is how many people who visited this page actually accepted the offer.

When you are clear on objective metrics like this, it makes measuring your marketing very simple. Not surprisingly, *many small business owners are scared of doing this, because it might reveal that their advertisements are not working.*

And that's the entire point!

When it comes to marketing, ignorance is not bliss.

In general, a good conversion percentage on your landing page is 10% or higher. 20% or higher is excellent. So, for every 100 unique visitors to your landing page, if you can get 10-20 to actually sign up and give you their contact info, that is a success. This means that if 80% implicitly say "no thanks," then that's fantastic!

It's actually good news.

This means that you've disqualified people that weren't

interested, and can now focus your time and money on prospects that are interested in what you have to offer them. They've proven so by trading you their contact information for your offer.

Do you see how this approach to marketing will radically simplify your life and eliminate the stress and frustration?

Stress comes from not knowing what to do. We don't get frustrated with long "to do" lists; rather, we get frustrated when we have open ended problems that we don't know how to solve.

Do you see the difference?

Stress is the direct result of ambiguity and confusion. And for most small business owners, the #1 source of confusion comes from trying to figure out what works and what doesn't work in their marketing.

Imagine how you would feel if you knew exactly what worked and what didn't work. Imagine how you would feel if you knew exactly how much it cost to you to "acquire" a customer.

Let's say after using landing pages for a couple days to measure your marketing, you discover that your average CPL is about $8. So, for every $40 you spend on advertising, you bring in about five new customers.

Here's where this gets fun…

Knowing your numbers means you can reverse engineer your business growth. You can actually *design* a strategy to grow your profits, in the same way an engineer designs a building. There is no guesswork or luck involved—it's simple 4th grade math.

Let's say you own a family restaurant, and the average receipt is about $35. You are expecting a slow month coming up, so you decide to run a measurable marketing campaign to boost traffic to the store. Your goal is 100 new customers, which represents about $3500 in gross revenues (restaurant margins are typically 30%ish, so $3500 gross is around $1000 of *profit*).

When you know your numbers, you can *design* profitable growth in your business.

If your marketing software reveals that your cost per lead is $8 (based on the landing page conversion), this means that you'd need to spend $800 to bring in 100 new customers. That $800 investment would create $3500 in new revenues for your business. And that's not even counting the future revenues from referrals, repeat customers, upsells like dessert/drinks, etc.

Imagine how easy it would be to run your small business if you could create a quick cash surge like this!

It all starts with knowing your numbers.

The easiest way to do this is by having marketing software do the work for you. Rather than having a messy desk full of random Post It notes and redeemed coupons, landing page software can keep track of everything for you (and automatically calculate the CPL of various ads).

Personally, I use *FrontDesk* software. It's the easiest small business marketing software to use, and it's surprisingly affordable. Just $32/month (you can check it out at www.tryfrontdesk.com).

Simplicity is very important here.

The more complicated you make your marketing system, the less likely you are to stick with it. That's why I use software—it does all the work for me. All you need to do is upload the images and text you want to use, and the software will automatically create landing pages, AND keep track of everyone that signs up.

Usually, it takes me less than 5 minutes to create a new landing page for an ad campaign.

It's almost a "secret weapon" of sorts. Using landing pages to measure your advertisements gives you an incredible advantage over your competitors. They have no idea if their ads are working, so they will continue to blindly waste money on advertisements that produce little to no results.

But if you're using landing pages to accurately track your marketing dollars, you will know *exactly* what your return on investment is.

This is a powerful advantage.

Using landing pages to measure your marketing will change your business forever.

Seriously.

You will be in control of your business, instead of your business controlling you!

Rather than guessing with ambiguous advertising, you will know if an ad worked. Using landing pages gives you ultimate clarity in your marketing.

Based on how many people sign up for your offer, you will know exactly, to the penny, what your CPL is for a given advertisement (cost per lead).

Did you spend $150 on a newspaper ad, and 24 people signed up for more information? The math is simple: on this particular advertisement your CPL was $6.25 (the 150 dollar advertisement divided by 24 new leads).

There is no right or wrong when it comes to a "good" cost per lead—that will be different for every business.

When it comes to "converting" the traffic into actual customers, anything below 10% means there is something wrong with the landing page (maybe a misleading headline, confusing picture, etc). That, or the advertisement itself was misleading, and tricked people into visiting your landing page.

This is why it's important to be honest in your advertising...there's no point in paying to send traffic to a landing page if you've used cheesy "bait and switch" tactics. That kind of cheap traffic won't *convert* into actual leads.

Raw website is traffic is overrated. The only thing that matters is how many people actually opted in!

Once you start using landing pages to accurately measure your marketing, your small business will never be the same.

Oh, and pat yourself on the back....

You just scored a hot date to the prom.

Idea Six: Marketing Is Like Dating, Part Two (How To Convince Someone To Marry You, Or At Least Get A Second Date)

So, she said "yes." You will be escorting Katie to the prom.

Nice work.

Now comes the hard part. What's your plan to convince her to actually date you? After all, going to a dance with someone doesn't constitute a relationship. If you aren't intentional about things, she may never say another word to you again.

If you want Katie to have your babies someday, we need to develop an actual relationship with her. This isn't one-time transaction. One night stands are overrated in life and in business. If you want true fulfillment, and true profits, you need to think about the long term.

How can we develop a mutually beneficial *relationship*

with our customers?

The truth about most businesses is that the real money is made on the "back end," NOT the initial transaction. So don't stress yourself out trying to create marketing campaigns that produce massive profits right away—this is very, very difficult to do.

The best strategy is to get them in the door with an irresistible offer, overdeliver on their expectations, and then cultivate a long-term relationship with them that will result in future purchases and referrals.

Remember: future purchases have higher margins, because there isn't a customer acquisition cost to account for!

If you're focused on generating new customers, most advertising campaigns will *not* be profitable the first time. Over the long run, however, they *will* be......if you develop a lasting relationship with those new customers.

Let's say you're in the mood for sex...

(How's that for a transitional sentence?!)

You *could* approach a beautiful woman, knock her over the head with a club, and get your sex that way. But you're not a rapist.

There's easier, more ethical ways of getting what you

want.

Unfortunately, most small business owners think like rapists.

Don't get me wrong; they are probably wonderful people, full of integrity. But they simply do not understand what it takes to build a long-term relationship with their clients.

- They *don't* follow up with leads.
- They *don't* thank their customers after purchases.
- They *don't* stay in touch with their customers on a regular basis.

They're the business equivalent of horny college kids who want to score with a different sorority girl every weekend.

This is no way to live, and it's no way to operate a business.

When we are looking for a mutually beneficial, long-term relationship with another human being, we do things *very* differently. It doesn't matter if we're talking about dating, business, or casual friendship.

Imagine that it's the morning after prom. You and Katie had a great time; she even let you kiss her on the cheek. Life is good.

You're going to call her today, right? I hope so.

Look at it from Katie's perspective. She took a risk going to prom with you. She didn't know you all that much, but you seemed like a nice guy. And, she really *did* have fun with you. You didn't try anything sketchy; you were a gentleman.

She is probably *waiting* for you to call her!

Assuming you've asked for her number (captured her contact information), now is the time for follow-up!

Nothing pushy, just a simple, "Hey Katie, I had a great time with you last night. Did you have fun?"

Proper follow-up *indirectly* communicates that you valued the initial experience with someone. You remember it. It was important to you. You want to remind the other person of that experience, and let them know you've been thinking of them.

All of this applies to business! It's so obvious, I don't even need to explain the similarities!

Human psychology is a constant, regardless of the context.

We are wired to react the same way whether we're in a romantic relationship or a business relationship. We want to be valued. We want people to acknowledge our existence.

What do you suppose Katie will think if a week goes by and she doesn't hear from you? What do you suppose Katie will think if a single *day* goes by and she doesn't hear from you?

So far in this book, I've mentioned a few actionable ideas you can apply to your business *right away* to start making more money. One of the easiest things you can do is commit to doing proper follow-up.

In the age of smartphones, it's never been easier.

Commit to sending a follow-up email after any interaction......*right away.* If you have a lunch meeting with a prospect at noon, and you're back at the office by 1:30, a follow-up email better be in their inbox by 1:31 PM.

This devotion to detail will make you stand out from the 95% of people that don't do this.

Little hinges swing big doors.

Something as simple as a follow-up email after a meeting sets the tone for a business relationship. Or a romantic one.

Here's the deal: successful people are successful because they are willing to do simple things like follow-up. They do it consistently, with no exceptions. It becomes a habit.

Simple things like follow up *really aren't hard to do.*

Proper follow-up is actually very *easy* to do.

It's also easy *not* to do, **and that's why most people never do it.**

Think back to Katie. Your willingness to call and "follow up" with her is the difference between her being your date to the senior prom and her potentially being your *wife.*

All of this because of a single phonecall.

Little hinges swing big doors.

Let's say you decide to get really creative. After calling her, you have flowers sent to her door *that same night,* with a handwritten card.

Inside the card, you include two tickets to the zoo, and a note that says, "Can I pick you up at 5 tomorrow evening?"

Multi-media, multi-step follow up. Yeah, baby.

I cannot tell you how often I've had business owners tell me that they're frustrated with their current marketing, because it's "not working."

Usually, I find out all they did was run *one* ad, send *one* postcard, send *one* email, etc. One is a bad number in business, especially in marketing.

Most advertising campaigns *require* multiple steps to be effective. Sure, every now and then you'll strike gold with a single postcard mailing or a single email or a single newspaper ad.

Exceptions prove the rule.

Think about it like this: the Allies would not have been victorious on D-Day if they gave up after the first wave of soldiers failed to secure the beach. No, no, no. It took multiple waves of attacks (and thousands of lives) to secure the beachhead.

It would have been silly to give up so easily.

Your business is no different.

My general rule is that your campaign should consist of *at least* two steps with the primary medium (direct mail, email, etc), while simultaneously featuring "touches" with secondary mediums.

Here's what I mean....

Let's say you own an appliance store. Grilling season is just around the corner, and you just got a big shipment of grills in. To engineer a spike in sales, you decide to send out a postcard to your customer database reminding people that summer is fast approaching (and they should buy a grill to celebrate!).

On a high margin item, a single postcard mailing *might*

pay for itself. If you spent $400 on printing and postage, it wouldn't take many sales to "break even" on your advertising costs.

However, when mailing to our in-house list of customers, the goal is never to break even. When we communicate a marketing message to our client list, we want to *make money!*

Here's how to do that: **send at least one follow up post card, and include multiple touches from different media other than postcards.**

So, 3-4 days after receiving the postcard, your clients should receive *another* postcard. The second one will repeat the offer, reference the first post card you sent (if they haven't looked at it yet, they will now!), ask them why they haven't responded to such a great deal, and encourage them to act *now* before the savings disappear.

Depending on the economics of what you're selling (ie you can afford to invest more in marketing if you're selling cars than if you're selling ice cream cones), you should always invest as much as you can into marketing.....and then invest a little bit more.

Continuously stretch your comfort zone.

Why? Well, you'll figure out pretty quickly that every additional "touch" in your marketing campaign increases sales.

For some strange reason, many customers will finally decide to buy after a second postcard, *that wouldn't have purchased with a single postcard.*

Many more will finally decide to take action after they receive a third postcard in the mail. These customers would not have purchased with only two postcards—for whatever reason, receiving the third postcard is what pushed them over the edge. It moved them to *take action.*

And the fourth postcard you send will convince even more of your customers to finally buy. Again, the customers that buy after the fourth postcard wouldn't have purchased with only three. Their purchase can be attributed to that 4th "touch."

Most business owners don't realize how close many customers are to actually buying. They *want* to buy a grill. They just need a little extra encouragement. You know, something to remind them of *how much* they want a grill.

Refusing to invest in multiple "touches" is cowardly. It shows that you aren't willing to spend a buck to earn five. Or, more realistically, spend a few hundred to earn a few thousand.

Or more.

Remember: **you will experience a measurable increase in sales for every additional step you build into a marketing campaign.**

Let's assume I've convinced you that it's a good idea to send a 3-step postcard campaign.

Would you like me to reveal the secret for *turbocharging* the success of your campaign?

There *is* a tactic you can use that almost guarantees your campaign will produce sizable profits.

This tactic is really easy. It is simple. And that's why most businesses won't do it!

They think to themselves, "That's beneath us. We're more sophisticated than that."

Friends, never be too proud to try something new—especially if what you're trying has been proven to produce results for other people in similar situations. What makes you think *your* business is different?

You've already invested some money into sending a 3-step postcard campaign. Now it's time to lock in your profits with the "secret weapon" of small business marketing.

First, a quick story....

I first stumbled onto this *secret weapon* while working on political campaigns.

I've volunteered, and served on paid staff, for multiple political candidates over the years. Here's *my* dirty little secret (don't tell anyone!): much of what I know about marketing I learned from the political world.

There are many "best practices" in political campaigns that can be applied to small business marketing. Likewise, many campaigns can learn a thing or two from the so-called private sector. Unfortunately, many campaign operatives have never worked in the business world, or vice-versa.

There are always profits to be had in identifying proven ideas in one industry and figuring out how those ideas apply to *your* industry.

If you know anything about politics, you know that campaigns are driven by image. They say that marketing is all about perception. Well, in politics, this is *literally* true.

In politics, reality is determined by the perception created by consultants like me. For example, when you design an event (notice the intentional usage of the word *design*), you take into consideration things like room size, lighting, acoustics, etc.

Campaign consultants want to make everything *look* and *feel* like a success. Everything from the camera angles to the temperature of a room contributes to how an event "feels." Live attendees want to experience excitement, but perhaps more importantly, events need to look successful for the folks watching on TV, and reading about it in the papers.

Where am I going with this?

Well, here's how this relates to small business marketing: you *must* commit to learning how to "design" successful marketing initiatives.

There really *is* a proven list of ingredients that goes into baking the perfect marketing cake. Don't fool yourself into thinking it's random chance.

It's not.

You can literally *design* a successful campaign in the same way an artist creates a painting. You just need to know where to put the brush.

While working with campaigns, I realized that events were much more successful when we promoted them with multiple media.

Not *slightly* more successful.

Not 10% more successful.

Not even 20% more successful.

More like 50% more successful, and in many cases, 100% more successful.

If all we did was email our list and say, "Hey everybody, we'll see you at the County Fair at 7 PM on Saturday," maybe *a few* people would show up (these were the hardcore supporters that would have showed up anyways).

However, I found that when we used a multiple step, multiple media approach, the success of our promotions increased exponentially.

For really important functions, we would send out *multiple* mailers, *multiple* emails, *multiple* mentions on social media, AND we'd make good old fashioned phone calls.....*multiple* times.

In this way, the average person on our list would be hearing from us in their email inbox, their physical mailbox, their Facebook newsfeed, *and* by their phone ringing.

To name just a few.

With a marketing campaign as "aggressive" as this, they can't help but think to themselves, "Wow, this event must be pretty important if they're mailing, emailing, AND calling me.

Maybe I'll check it out."

When you have hundreds (or thousands) of your prospects having this internal dialogue in their heads, a pretty good percentage of them will eventually choose to take action.

Don't think of your target market as a bunch of people. Think about it as one person.

If your marketing campaign was being delivered to *one person*, and the entire objective was to get that *one person* to buy from you, would you do things differently?

Probably.

That *one person* is much more likely to respond if we send them multiple mailers, multiple emails, multiple phone calls, etc.

Especially if each "touch" is unique….

Here's what I mean: **don't make the second mailer identical to the first.**

- Use a different size card.
- Larger.
- Smaller.
- Different shape.
- Different paper stock (thickness or texture).
- Different copy.

Maybe don't send a postcard; send a 3-page letter. Or a poster.

Just because you sent a postcard the first time doesn't mean you have to send another identical postcard.

Keep them guessing.

This principle applies beyond a specific marketing campaign. It's also true for the overall relationship you are nurturing with prospects and customers.

I started this chapter by emphasizing the importance of follow up; specifically, implementing multiple media follow up.

There's a big difference between a first date and a marriage. The difference is creativity. The difference is commitment.

The difference is follow up.

So, in summary, the "secret weapon" missing from most marketing campaigns (and single men) is multiple media follow up.

You will amplify the results of any promotion by using postcards AND phonecalls, postcards AND emails, postcards AND TV commercials, postcards AND radio ads, etc.

Ideally, use *everything*.

Your budget is the only limitation.

And, really, budget shouldn't be an excuse. It might be more accurate to say your *imagination* is the only limitation.

If the economics "work," your profits will increase with every additional dollar you invest in your marketing campaign. Don't think of additional mailers or phone calls as *expenses.*

They are *investments.*

Every dollar you invest will create multiple dollars flowing back into your business. THAT is the essence of good marketing.

So, commit to following up with Katie. She *wants* you to call her. She *wants* to get to know you. She *wants* to take things to the next level.

Surprise her.

Delight her.

Because marketing is like dating.

Idea Seven: Marketing Is Like Friendship

Do you have any friends that you've lost touch with?

Maybe you were best friends in high school, or college roommates.

You did everything together. Spring break trips, summer vacations, weekend movies. You swore you'd never drift apart.

When everyone else grew up, found real jobs, got married and had kids, you and your friends would stay in contact. You would beat the odds. You would be the exception.

Because your friendship was special. It was different. It would last!

Until it didn't.

Almost all of us can look back and remember "best friends" that are now almost completely absent from our lives. Nothing drastic occurred. Our lives go in different directions (sometimes figuratively, sometimes geographically).

We slowly drift apart. It's no one's fault.

Life happens.

What's peculiar about this is that all it would take to

"maintain" a friendship is a little effort.

Nothing terribly time consuming, just enough communication to let the other person know you didn't forget about their existence. A little bit goes a long way.

- A five minute "how are you doing" phone call once a month.
- An annual invitation to dinner or a sporting event.
- An email every now and then.
- Maybe an occasional letter.

If you *really* valued the friendship, you would make the effort. Because, let's be honest with ourselves, it wouldn't take much.

When a friendship already exists, there's no inertia to overcome. There is momentum. All we have to do is keep it from slowing down to an eventual standstill.

But that's what *usually happens.*

Why is this?

In business and in life, most of us are willing to exert much more effort creating something from scratch than we are maintaining it.

Marketing is like friendship.

Think about how much time you spend developing a new friendship from scratch. Now consider how much time you allocate to "maintenance" of those friendships.

Is there an imbalance? Probably.

Most of us don't want to put any additional time or energy into the preservation of our relationships. We neglect them over and over again, until one day our best friends are little more than acquaintances.

Marketing is like friendship.

How many resources do you devote to strengthening the relationship you have with your customers? Not prospects, but customers.

People that have *already* bought from you.

Most businesses will spend a lot of money acquiring *new* customers. They'll constantly advertise on the radio, in the newspaper, and wherever else they think potential customers will "discover" them.

Then when their advertising actually works—and new prospects become paying customers—they all but ignore them.

Big mistake.

- There is no effort made to thank the customer.
- There is no effort made to offer the customer

further value.

- There is no effort made to make the customer feel special.

In fact, it's usually the opposite. Most businesses focus ALL of their advertising on acquiring new customers. They give perks for new customers. They give the best deals to new customers. They roll out the red carpet for new customers.

When was the last time you gave your *existing* clients the VIP treatment? When was the last time you singled them out for being great customers, and gave them a special deal to thank them for supporting you?

At a bare minimum, when was the last time you communicated with them without trying to sell them something?

Let's get specific here: your business should be sending out a print newsletter every single month to your customer list. Period.

Not an email newsletter. A physical print newsletter (the kind that the United States Postal Service delivers to physical mailboxes).

In this informal newsletter, talk about what's going on in your personal life. Did you recently take your family on vacation to Mexico? Write about it! Include some pictures of you on vacation, and a short write up of how the trip went. Your fans will *love* hearing about your personal life. It's refreshing to open up a piece of mail and not immediately be barraged with a sales message.

Because, let's face it, most of us are inundated with spammy sales messages all day long. That's no fun.

What's worse, we've come to expect it!

A great way to stand out is to communicate with no strings attached.

Your customers will breathe a sigh of relief after reading through a letter from you that didn't conclude with a massive sales pitch. Or start with one.

This doesn't mean you can't occasionally mention promotions or special offers in your newsletters, just that they should be the exception—not the rule.

If you can resist the temptation to include a commercial pitch in every piece of communication that goes out, the instances where you *do* try to sell something will be much more effective.

In fact, people will be *glad* to buy from you….because they know, like, and trust you.

You proved to them you weren't looking to make a quick buck.

Think about it: when was the last time your car dealer, dentist, or insurance agent sent you a letter talking about what's going on in their "personal" life?

Do you have any idea what your car dealer's hobbies are? What recent vacations he took? Whether his children are involved with extracurricular activities? His political opinions? What church he goes to? His favorite baseball team? His favorite place in town to get a cheeseburger?

When you communicate personal information to your customer list—the same type of stuff you would chat about with your buddies—they will begin to view you as a friend.

A trusted resource.

When you nurture *that* type of relationship, two important things will happen that change the entire dynamic of your business:

1. Customer loyalty strengthens to cult-like levels.
2. Referrals seemingly happen out of nowhere.

Again, all you need to do is commit to staying in touch with your customers after they buy from you. In my opinion, there is no better way to do this than a print newsletter, delivered to their mailbox every month.

Show them that you actually care!

Marketing is like friendship.

Nurture an authentic friendship with your clients. It doesn't matter if you're selling insurance or gym memberships, it's basic human psychology that makes this work.

If you want to increase the lifetime value of your customers AND get them to refer their friends to you, proceed as if you're trying to maintain one of those aforementioned college friendships. Forget for a moment that this is a profit-driven enterprise.

Think of them as friends. Not customers.

No more one night stands. We want long-term customers that refer their friends!

Most businesses can increase their profits without investing any additional money on marketing. They just need to *allocate* it differently.

Let's say your database of customers has about 300 names in it. Commit RIGHT NOW to mailing them a monthly print newsletter. It will cost you about $150 per month with printing and postage, and it will be the best marketing dollars you invest.

Trust me on this one.

Every dollar you invest in acquiring new customers is a complete waste of money if you aren't prepared to invest in maintaining those relationships.

Besides, *it's much, much, much cheaper to get existing customers to buy more from you than it is to get complete strangers to check you out for the first time.*

Every dollar in sales that is generated by advertising to the general public could have been two or three dollars in sales if the advertising had been focused on pre-existing customers.....people that *already* know, like, and trust you.

When you communicate with your existing family of customers (Seth Godin refers to it as a "tribe"), the hard work is already done!!!

They already *know* you.

They already *like* you.

And they already *trust* you.

At this point, marketing stuff is almost easy.

In the context of a real relationship, recommending valuable solutions to people's problems is actually *welcome.* You are not an annoying pest; you are a welcomed guest. Your family of customers is eager to learn about how you can solve their problems.

This pre-existing trust does *not* exist with the general public.

Marketing is like friendship.

Think about this for a second: when you meet somebody for the first time, do you immediately invite them to go on vacation with you? Probably not.

That would be weird, and awkward.

Traveling with someone is usually reserved for relationships where we have known the other person for quite some time.

If you've just met somebody, maybe the friendship will develop over lunches together, grabbing coffee every now and then, or watching football games every Sunday afternoon.

We usually don't invite someone we just met to tag along on our family road trip. It's too much, too fast.

If we wouldn't act this way in our personal lives, why do we do it in business?

Why do so many businesses immediately blast out promotional offers to the general public without first establishing a relationship with people?

Before you make "the ask," you must first educate the

customer and develop a relationship. This is usually a process, and doesn't happen overnight.

If you're communicating with "cold" leads that have no prior relationship with you (ie, a rented mailing list or an ad in the newspaper), you should focus on making "low threshold" offers that are designed to do one thing and one thing only: generate leads.

Which is another way of saying, "Make friends."

Do not expect your ad to take someone all the way from being casually interested to actually purchasing your product. For most products, this doesn't work.

Don't ask for sex on the first date. Or bend down on one knee and pop the question. It's intimidating, and rather stupid. Embarrassing, really.

And it's why most advertising you're probably running right now isn't working.

Instead, focus on appealing to their pre-existing interest, stimulating that interest, and then offering them a free, zero-pressure way to respond. This is the essence of a "low threshold" offer.

It is commonly referred to as a lead-generation ad.

The goal of a lead generation ad is self-explanatory:

generate leads. You're not trying to make any sales; your objective is getting as many people as possible to raise their hands and say, "Hey, I'm interested in that!"

It's about building your list of prospects.

If you know that on average, ten percent of prospects will eventually become customers, it's simply a game of math. If you have ten prospects, you will get one actual sale. If you have one hundred, you'll get ten sales.

This isn't rocket science.

Once you figure this out (the math is different for every type of business), **making more money is as easy as building your list.** Ten percent of 500 is more than ten percent of 100. Or whatever your typical conversion ratio happens to be.

There is a huge difference between the ads most businesses run and the ads they should be running. This can be the difference between success and failure. Riches and poverty.

If you grasp this concept, you can turn around your business in a week or less.

Let's explore this further....

There are high-threshold offers and there are low-threshold offers.

High threshold offers are scary, intimidating, and

involve a certain level of commitment. High threshold offers will only appeal to people that are ready to buy, right now.

Or are almost ready to buy.

They will alienate everyone else who may be interested *but is not ready to make any type of commitment*, or be put in a sales situation where they will be pressured into making a decision.

Examples of high threshold offers would include financial advisors offering "free consultations," car dealers promoting "test drives," and timeshare hucksters advertising hard-sell presentations disguised as "free dinners."

If you're only casually interested in a new car, you probably don't want to schedule a test drive with a commission-motivated salesman struggling to meet his monthly quota.

But you *would* be interested in a free report on "3 Little Known Secrets to Negotiating A Better Deal On Your Next Used Car Purchase."

This is the essence of a lead generation ad. It's *low threshold*, meaning it doesn't involve a ton of commitment from the prospect. It's not intimidating. Fear of a hard-sell sales presentation won't prevent them from visiting a website to download their free report. You've provided a low-pressure "first step."

It allows them to engage with you without feeling like they have to make any type of commitment. They are learning about how you can solve their problems while simultaneously establishing a relationship with them—a relationship *voluntarily initiated by the prospect!*

They will actually welcome additional follow up because *they initiated the friendship.*

Infusing your advertising with low threshold, "lead generation" offers will make your current ad dollars EXPONENTIALLY more effective.

Most ads imply direct offers, asking customers to buy something. Right now.

I'm not against this—it's certainly better than the vague "branding" bullshit peddled by many ad salesmen.

Unfortunately, this type of advertising only appeals to people at the "bottom" of the sales funnel.....those ready to buy, *right now*. These ads ignore the vast majority of interested prospects that want to find out more about your product, but they are not ready to buy something...or endure an intimidating sales presentation.

To generate more revenue without buying more ads, make the ads you *do* run work harder for you. Invest in "low-threshold," lead generation advertising.

Like I've said, it's ALWAYS cheaper to generate sales by communicating with your "friends." People that already know you, like you, and trust you.

Your existing database.

Once a relationship is developed, "selling" feels a lot more like "prescribing." It doesn't come across as sleazy, like you're trying to make a quick buck off of ignorant strangers.

When you've developed a genuine relationship with your customers, they *want* you to give them advice about what will make their lives easier. They *want* you to solve their problems.

Think about the last time you went to the doctor....

Did you get defensive when he or she prescribed certain medications, or recommended therapy? Subconsciously, you know that medical professionals make a lot of money. This doctor is being paid hundreds of dollars an hour to consult with you. He or she is *definitely* selling you something.

But no one thinks of the doctor as a "salesperson." Why is that?

The answer is pretty simple, but it's profound. The implications for small business marketing are HUGE.

Before we explore the actual dynamic that makes this possible, be sure to recognize a secondary principle here: when you notice something in life that "works" really well, train yourself to think: how can I make this work for *my* business?

Examples abound all around us of interesting business models, pricing strategies, marketing campaigns, and unique advertising messages that are making people lots of money in *their* industry.

Begin borrowing these strategies and ways of thinking, and put them to work for *your* business.

Let's take another look at how doctors subconsciously "market" themselves...

Doctors have positioned themselves (and rightfully so) as experts that are prescribing solutions to people's problems.

Here's what makes this work: medical professionals are not selling a product; they are prescribing a solution. Not selling, *prescribing*. Not a product, but a *solution*.

Because they are perceived as being experts that simply want to solve our problems, **they are able to charge very high fees without ever encountering price resistance** (On an interesting side note, the business model/price strategy of using prepaid insurance premiums makes it much easier for the health care industry to charge *incredibly* high prices. Think of ways to apply this to your business—it is possible!).

When was the last time you told a doctor, "Nah, that's too expensive. Maybe I'll go to the discount doctor down the road for a cheaper alternative."

Ha!

This would *never* happen, because we've been conditioned to accept the doctor's prescriptions as gospel truth. Even though we don't know them, we *trust* them.

Most of us wouldn't consider the doctor to be our friend, but we accept their advice just the same. We genuinely believe that they want what is best for us, so we listen to their advice and act on it.

And we pay the bill without complaining, or shopping around for the "best deal."

I'm not criticizing doctors here, I'm merely pointing out the marketing genius behind the psychology of this interaction.

Marketing is like friendship.

What can we learn from the *positioning* of doctors? Can this strategy of authority and trust be applied to other "normal" businesses like vacuum cleaner sales?

Yes, it can.

First, we must recognize that marketing is like friendship. And that's a different way of saying that marketing simply recognizes the psychology that drives human interaction, and leverages these psychological dynamics in a way that's profitable for our businesses.

The reason that proper marketing principles "work" regardless of the business or industry they're applied in is that ALL industries and businesses have ONE thing in common: human beings.

Specifically, human beings with psychological desires and needs.

It doesn't matter what we're selling—vacuum cleaners or vasectomies. Human psychology is what drives people to desire certain outcomes, and take action to achieve those outcomes.

If I could go back and pick a different major in college, it would definitely be psychology (I studied economics and finance). A proper understanding of psychology is the foundation of good marketing.

The field of "economics" tends to reduce human

purchasing behavior to mathematically-driven, rational calculations. In reality, it's much more complex than that. No one is purely "rational" in a mathematical or logical sense.

After all, we all know that buying things on credit isn't very smart.

We all know that it's better to save up for things and pay cash.

We all know that avoiding consumer debt is important.

We all know that Cheesecake Factory will not help us maintain a 6-pack.

Success in life—whether financial, relational, or medical—is driven by our understanding of the psychology of decision-making.

And how disciplined we are at actually *applying* the wisdom we already possess!

They say that technology is simply "applied science."

Imagine a world where everyone was an academic theorist, but nobody bothered to apply any of the discoveries into practical solutions for everyday problems.

This is the difference between engineers and entrepreneurs, scientists and salesmen. To actually benefit from new knowledge, we must first apply it. If we didn't, we'd have electricity—but no light bulbs. Fire, but no combustible engines.

Science, but no technology.

It's not exactly a "secret" that losing weight is as simple as exercising a little bit more and eating a little bit less. It's not a lack of knowledge that makes us fat. It's not even a lack of knowledge that makes us poor.

It is a lack of *applying* knowledge that condemns us to a life of mediocrity.

When it comes to marketing, we must first understand that marketing is simply convincing people to take action on something.

We're all marketers.

Since we were little kids, we've been trying to convince people of things. Some people call it "persuasion."

Well, marketing is just the systemization of persuasion.

That's it.

Marketing is examining what makes certain arguments and ideas persuasive, and figuring out how to scale that persuasion to appeal to the masses.

If I were to explain the concept of marketing to a five year old, I would say, "Marketing is telling people why they should do stuff."

Not too complicated, right?

Remember: marketing is like friendship.

Marketing is like friendship because friends trust the recommendations of their friends. Re-read that sentence a few times until it sinks in.

The overall goal of any marketing strategy is developing prospects into friends—people that know you, like you, and trust you. Because people that know you, like you, and trust you.....will *buy* from you.

And tell *their* friends to do the same.

If you are good at marketing, you'll have a lot of "friends."

This is crucially important for the success of a locally-owned small business. There is much less persuasion needed in the context of a friendship. Which is another way of saying you will end up spending less money on marketing.

Well, more accurately, you'll stop wasting money on *stupid* marketing that you can then redirect into *measurable* marketing.

Which is another way of saying, "You'll make more money."

And it all begins with building relationships with your target market. Going out and making friends. Getting people to know you, like you, and trust you.

For example, when a friend invites you to go see a movie, you are not suspicious of ulterior motives.

"Will he profit off of this somehow? What's in it for him? Is the movie theater giving him some sort of kickback, a commission, for bringing me to the movies tonight? Maybe I will just stay home..."

Yeah right!

You would probably just say, "Yeah, that sounds like fun. Let's do it. See you there at 7."

However, when a sales rep invites you out for lunch, you immediately know that there is an ulterior motive. You *expect* a sales pitch. You have to be bribed by a free lunch to even agree to the meeting!

This is not a very efficient way to sell stuff.

Nor is it any fun.

Do you think sales people enjoy being viewed as "the annoying sales rep?" Hell no. This is a psychologically traumatic way to make a living. It's prostitution sans sex.

Making friends is easier, more fun, and more profitable.

Friendship is really just the word we use to describe the point in a relationship where we know, like, and trust somebody. We assume that they want what's best for us. We don't question their motives. We enjoy their company, and we trust their recommendations.

Your goal should be to convert as many of your "prospects" as you can into friends.

When large amounts of people view you as a trusted resource—a friend—they will go to you when they have a problem they believe you can solve. They will trust your recommendation. They won't haggle on price. They won't shop around.

An understanding of psychology is what enables this process to take place.

And, really, if you understand psychology, implementing various marketing processes is simply a process of deduction.

Earlier in this chapter, I mentioned a specific marketing "technology." A tactic that resulted from understanding social psychology, and *applying* the knowledge to the business world: **a monthly print newsletter.**

I want to quickly reiterate the importance of having some sort of monthly communication with your "friends."

Friends stay in touch.

Friends provide value without expecting something in return.

Friends produce monthly newsletters.

If you're not sending out a monthly newsletter right now, start yesterday. It's perhaps the easiest—and cheapest—thing you can do to stimulate sales RIGHT NOW.

When I assist in producing newsletters for clients, I usually have the first 90% or so of the newsletter be "personal stuff" about what's going on in the life of the business owner. Recent vacations they took, a really good grade their kid got on their most recent report card, what their favorite drink is at the local coffee shop, etc. The goal is to give the customers a glimpse into the "real" you.

Even if they've never met you in person, they should feel like they know you after being on your business's mailing list for a few months and reading your newsletters.

They should know the names of your family members, what kind of dog you have, what school your kids go to, and the most recent novel you read. They should feel like they have a personal connection with you. You are their *friend*.

Prospects and existing customers should look forward

to opening your mail and reading it.

Is that true of the current crap you're blasting out to your mailing list?

Do customers actually look forward to reading your blatant hard-sell advertising? Do they eagerly anticipate monthly mailbox rape (forcing a sales presentation onto someone who never asked for it)?

Like I said, it's not as if you cannot include some sort of offer in your communication. In fact, you *should.* But it shouldn't *feel* like a sales letter.

When producing newsletters for my clients, I like to hint towards an offer at the end of the letter.....*at the beginning of the letter.* Ideally, in the first paragraph. Maybe even the first sentence.

Sometimes a newsletter starts like this:

"Hey Tom, I hope you're having a wonderful summer. I know I am. In fact, to celebrate how great of a summer we've had, I want to extend a special offer to you. I'll reveal the specifics at the end of the letter. But for now, let me tell you why I'm in such a good mood (besides the fact that it's sunny and 75 outside right now!). I recently took my kids to the beach for a lake day. Late in the afternoon, after we were all burnt to

a crisp and ready to pack up and drive home, my oldest son told me something that I'll never forget…."

The first thing you probably noticed is that this does not feel at all like a typical business newsletter. Most of the horsecrap that small businesses mail their clients is sales pitch after sales pitch after sales pitch.

The second subtle tactic here is that I hinted at something special waiting for the reader at the end of the letter. This creates a burning desire in their mind to find out what it is.

I've created suspense.

I've created a "curiosity gap."

The plot of every narrative (whether it's a book, movie, or HBO miniseries) follows this psychological pattern: *develop some tension……resolve the tension.*

You can apply this trick within your newsletters!

Doing this gives the reader a reason to read the letter in its entirety (Sometimes these can be ten pages long or *more*. Remember, if you are actually entertaining the reader and providing value, they will keep reading. There's no metaphysical law of nature that says a letter sent from a business needs to be one page or less. In fact, more is better!).

Many times, your readers will actually skip to the end to read the "offer." It's just human nature to be impatient and want what we cannot have (no worries, they'll usually go back and read the whole letter).

In fact, readers will usually skip to the end anyway, read the "P.S.," read any subtitles, or highlighted sentences, and *then* decide whether the letter is worth reading.

Write your copy accordingly.

Human beings don't like waiting (this is just a small example of applying the knowledge of social psychology to our marketing efforts).

Can you think of any other scenarios where customers *can't wait* to be exposed to a promotional offer?!

That's pretty hard to replicate.

Be personal in your newsletter. Make it obvious that *you* wrote this newsletter, not some intern, or worse, a newsletter company.

Most business owners do not understand the importance of the personal connection. Without the personal connection, you might as well not waste your time doing this (or spend the money on postage).

Fortunately for *you*, dear reader, most businesses fail miserably in communicating with their customers.

If they do send an actual "newsletter," it's usually a template they bought from some marketing company that doesn't have anything to do with their personal lives or local community. Crossword puzzles, word finds, national news stories.

It clearly was not written by the business owner.

When the envelope is addressed from you, customers expect that *you* actually took the time to sit down and write them a letter!

Friends would expect that from their friends.

Do you "outsource" your friendships? That would be absurd. Nobody hires an Indian customer support center to manage their *personal* relationships. Why would you outsource your *business* communication?

It feels cheap, sleazy, and commercial. Don't be a prostitute. Or worse, a mailbox rapist.

Like I said, you can include offers in your newsletters. But at no point should the reader feel as if the purpose of the letter is to sell them something.

If you follow this rule, the cases where you *are* making

a direct attempt to sell something will be much more effective!

The context of a personal relationship is the key. This is what makes this tactic so ridiculously effective: friends view their friendships differently than consumers view the typical "I'm the seller, you're the buyer" dynamic.

Friends are friends because they give us intrinsic satisfaction. The joy of a friendship isn't in the measurable benefits it provides; it is its own reward.

Your customers should never feel like they are being "marketed" to. They should feel like valued friends.

They should look forward to receiving physical mail from you.

They should look forward to opening your emails.

They should look forward to attending your live events.

Marketing is like friendship.

Idea Eight: Marketing Is Like High School

It's all about packaging and positioning.

Remember high school?

Whether you were a nerd, athlete, or band geek, you probably remember the emotional roller coaster of your teenage years. High school is where we learn geometry, biology, and American history; it is also where our social habits are developed and ingrained for the rest of our lives.

If you think back to your glory days and conclude that you're wiser, more mature, and have "grown up" since then.....you are wrong.

Marketing is like high school.

The Darwinian social environment in most high schools is not a phase.

It's not something you escape.

You can't grow out of it.

You don't "mature" into a wiser human being, immune from making hollow value judgments based on people's clothing, hairstyle, or car.

According to the pop punk band *Bowling for Soup*, "High School Never Ends."

They are right.

Here's the deal: there are biological reasons why we act the way we do—especially in groups. This pattern of behavior takes root during adolescence, and never leaves us.

We might *think* that high school was a brutal time, that it was cutthroat, that we're more "civilized" as adults, that because we're older we don't judge people by the clothes they wear or the car they drive.

We are in denial.

Human beings are not purely rational, logical thinkers.

We make decisions emotionally, and then attempt to justify our emotional decisions with logic (to make ourselves feel better). This process plays out in nearly every decision we make.

Marketing is like high school.

If you believe that you are a descendant of Spock and are able to somehow make decisions in a logical vacuum, ask yourself: what kind of car do you drive? When did you last eat out at a restaurant? Do you own any clothes that are more expensive than thrift store fare?

Not that accumulating "stuff" is a bad thing. Far from it. But *logically*, we should be saving and investing all of our surplus dollars beyond what is necessary for basic sustenance.

It makes no *logical* sense to drive a Cadillac when it's basically a Chevy with the price tag doubled. It makes no *logical* sense to pay for bottled water. Much of what we do makes no *logical* sense, yet we do it anyways.

Because certain things make us happy. They make us *feel* good.

They cannot be rationalized with cold, hard logic.....but we still try.

Most decisions are made almost exclusively via emotion. We choose A over B because of how it will make us *feel.*

Subconsciously, we realize that the decision was made without ever consulting the logical side our brains. So we conjure up silly rationalizations as to why we did what we did.

"Well, I actually get 30 miles per gallon with the new Cadillac CTS, so I save money every month on gas compared to my old truck" (never mind that the Caddy had a price tag of fifty grand, which will never be recovered in miniscule gas savings).

"I'm going to order the brownie sundae for dessert. Sometimes you just gotta live a little! No worries, I'll go for a run when we get home tonight" (never mind that the dessert has 700 calories, which you would need to run about seven miles to burn off).

"Yeah, our ten day vacation to Maui was pretty damn expensive—maybe we shouldn't have flown first class—but now that I've cleared my mind a bit, I'll be much more productive at work" (never mind that you could have simply taken a long weekend at a nearby resort and accomplished the same thing).

See the pattern here?

The first step is actually acknowledging that *you* make decisions emotionally. Don't be in denial about this. The sooner you recognize it for what it is, you can start applying this principle to your marketing.

As they say in high school, *everyone is doing it.*

Once you accept the fact that YOU make decisions emotionally, things become crystal clear.

Marketing becomes as simple as "What do people *really* want? What is *really* making them choose? Let's appeal to *that* in our messaging."

This goes beyond the traditional "features versus benefits" advertising maxim you've probably heard before.

Appealing to the true desires, the *primal urges* in all of us (love, sex, fear, etc), takes us deeper into the human psyche than features or benefits ever could.

Stop and think about it....

1. **Features** are descriptions of what a product *has* for us.

2. **Benefits** are descriptions of what a product *does* for us.

3. **Primal desires** explain *why* we want that result in the first place.

Once you realize that our primal desires to be accepted and valued by others drive all other "surface" wants, creating marketing messaging is a piece of cake.

It's worth repeating: **we make decisions emotionally, and then attempt to justify those decisions afterwards with logical rationalizations.**

We don't want others (or ourselves) to think that we lack self-control and are ruled by our emotions; therefore, we always make sure to explain our decisions with culturally acceptable, "logical" reasons.

We want to be accepted by society. We want to be valued by society. It goes without saying that we want our lifestyle decisions *and purchases* to be accepted and valued by society!

Imagine for a moment that you just bought a beautiful, million-dollar lake home. You are mortgaged to the point of monthly bankruptcy, but somehow you find a way to make the payment month after month.

Word spreads around the office that you just dropped a million bucks on a lakefront estate. Your apparent extravagance dominates all water cooler discussion.

When a few of your coworkers ask you about it, you say, "Well, I've always wanted people to think I was successful. I want people to look at me in admiration. As a child, my dad seldom told me he loved me, so I want to show the world that I'm worthy of affection. I bought the lake home as a symbol of my value."

In reality, we would probably brush it off and talk about how we got a great deal on the property, and didn't actually pay that much. We would say we've always wanted to live on the lake, and this deal was so good we simply couldn't pass it up.

In other words, we would attempt to justify our decision to those around us. **Even though we bought the lake home as a status symbol of our financial wealth**, we attempt to rationalize it with the *exact opposite* line of reasoning: we bought it because it was affordable.

Again, this post-decision rationalization occurs for two reasons:

1. We need to justify the emotional decision to ourselves
2. We need to justify the emotional decision to the world

If you gave the real answer as to why you bought the lake house (or foreign luxury sedan, expensive vacation, etc), people would think you're a selfish asshole with an out-of-control inferiority complex.

Such is the paradox of social psychology and human decision-making. Marketing *is* like high school.

Now that you understand the real psychological reasons behind our behavior, how will you change your marketing?

Your messaging?

Your pricing?

Your unique selling proposition?

Let's say you own a small gym, with less than 100

members.

The bigger players in your industry have a much larger marketing budget than you. Their fitness centers are open 24 hours with keyless entry. Their price strategy follows a low margin, high volume philosophy. They make a little money off of large amounts of members. They do this primarily by buying big advertisements in newspapers, radio, and occasionally local TV, bragging about how inexpensive they are.

Because they are owned by a big, dumb corporation (with very few exceptions, I am convinced that the larger an organization grows, the dumber it becomes), their advertising message is almost completely focused on features.

Not primal desire. Not even benefits, but stinkin *features.*

Fortunately for you, they haven't bothered to learn anything about human psychology. They think marketing is as easy as broadcasting that they have the cheapest price.

Like I said, they're a big dumb corporation.

While you may have fewer resources, a worse location, and a lesser-known "brand," you are in a good position here.

Trust me.

Because Goliath has staked his claim as the big dumb

corporate gym with low prices, *you can now position yourself as the exact opposite*: a smaller, community-oriented gym for those that take fitness really seriously—and are willing to pay a premium for it.

Let's say the big-box fitness center prices its memberships at $25/month. If it were me, I'd price mine at $60 a month *or higher.*

The farther away you are from their price point, the less people will view you as competition. If you're only *slightly* more expensive (the mistake most small businesses make), people will subconsciously think to themselves that your gym is a bad deal. After all, it costs more!

This is because you would be competing for the same market share as the big-box fitness center: the low cost gym.

If you price yourself much, much higher than the 24-hour fitness centers, people won't even compare you.

They'll mentally categorize you as *a different product entirely.*

For example, no one compares a Motel 6 to a Four Seasons resort. No one would ever complain to Four Seasons that they're too expensive, because "I stayed in a Motel 6 last night for only fifty bucks!"

This would be laughable.

Clearly, Four Seasons is an entirely different product than Motel 6. Both are hospitality businesses that involve paying a nightly fee for a bedroom, but they occupy completely different price points in the hospitality market—so much so, that no one would *dare* compare them.

They are so different, AND PRICED SO DIFFERENT, that consumers view them as *completely separate products* with absolutely nothing in common.

In fact, consumers are more likely to price shop the cost of sleeping in a tent at a campground than they are to compare an evening at a Motel 6 to a Four Seasons experience.

In the case of our locally owned gym, I would seek to dominate the market for *premium* fitness club memberships. Don't even bother with those who think it's too expensive.

Our target market here isn't necessarily affluent, but they really, truly care about fitness. They are willing to pay double (or more) for their gym membership to be apart of a fitness community that cares as much about lifting weights as they do.

When I write the copy for our various advertisements, sales letters, and follow up sequences, I would try to talk about the "primal desires" as much as possible.

Because I know beyond the shadow of a doubt that **consumers make decisions emotionally and then justify those decisions with clever rationalizations**, the message would be almost completely emotionally driven.

I'd throw in a few "logical" nuggets here and there so prospects can internally rationalize the cost of our gym membership, but the main driver of our message would revolve around appealing to primal desires.

Instead of defaulting to bragging about price, I would point out how great it *feels* to be in awesome shape, and what that says about you.

A sales letter for this gym might sound something like this:

*"It feels great to **be in control** of your body, to be in amazing shape.*

Not 'pretty good' shape like the neighbor who gets up early everyday to walk his dog. Or your coworkers that haphazardly do a few sets of bench press once a week. Or your second cousin that thinks he's Arnold Schwarzenegger because he drinks a protein shake every day.

*We're talking about being in peak physical condition. Visible abs. Defined shoulder muscles. **An almost superhuman physique**.*

It's not just about being able to deadlift five hundred pounds, *or bench press twice your body weight. It's the feeling of knowing **you can face whatever life throws at you**.....and win.*

You are a conqueror. And you enjoy every minute of the conquest.

Most people complain about going to workout, but as a member of our gym, you are the type of person that complains about <u>missing a workout.</u>

Others envy your discipline, your devotion, your borderline obsession with physical fitness. What they don't realize is that it's not physical—it's mental.

It's spiritual.

It's about being a different sort of person altogether.

It's about waking up before everyone else to fit your workout in.

It's about going to the gym even when you don't feel like it.

It's about making hard decisions.

Being a member of this gym says something about you. It says to the world that you are not content with average. It says that you are more afraid of mediocrity than you are of failure.

*It says you're willing to pay the price—financially and emotionally—to be the best you can be. **If this describes you**, you probably don't fit in at the other places in town. But we're different. We're just like you. We want more out of our gym membership because we want more out of life itself.*

Call today or visit our website to get started and discover the real you that is waiting to be unleashed.

Very intentionally, the words used in this ad are designed to attract a certain type of person and repel all others. Notice there is not even a *hint* of price in this message—it's all about communicating value; specifically, the primal desires that cause people to want to be in great shape in the first place.

The truth is that if you can connect your audience with their innermost, deepest desires, **they will pay almost any price for what you're offering.**

The key is to make sure what you're selling appeals to their primal desires! After all, the gym itself isn't what they're buying; they are buying alpha-male status.

They are buying the *confidence* that comes with being in above average physical condition.

They are buying the *looks* they'll get from girls at the beach.

They're definitely not buying something as boring and uninspiring as a *gym membership.*

Ask yourself: what is YOUR business *really* selling?

We all want to fit in. And in certain ways, we want to

stand out (like being in really good shape).

Marketing is like high school.

Most of the time, the problem isn't that a business is failing at delivering value. The problem is that they completely fail to *communicate* the true value of what they deliver.

If you think back to high school, you can probably rattle off the names of a few rich kids that always had the newest clothes, gadgets, and drove a brand new car.

Other than winning the sperm lottery, these kids did absolutely nothing to earn their "stuff." When you're 16, you haven't done jack shit to create value in the real world.

I'll spare you from a personal rant, but our culture prevents young people from contributing any value whatsoever to society. No wonder many of them go off to college and have no flipping clue what they want to do with their lives...they've never really done anything with their lives up to that point!

High school kids today play sports, maybe work a part time job fifteen hours a week, and then spend the rest of their time complaining about how much homework they don't actually have.

They have no real responsibilities other than waking up in time for school on weekdays.

For the first twenty years (sometimes longer) of most kids' lives, they live in a state of almost pure consumption. Their shelter is paid for by their parents, their food is paid for by their parents, and most of their clothing is covered by mom and dad, too.

What little they might produce—perhaps flipping burgers at the local shake shack—is usually just for extra spending money.

We've got to figure out a way to empower our young people to actually contribute value to society. They will be better off for it.

The way I see it, most American kids forfeit a decade or more of their lives to our antiquated, industrial-age education system. These are valuable years they will never get back, and the economic opportunity cost is incredibly high.

The cumulative effects of robbing a generation of the opportunity to contribute value should not be underestimated.

We've inflicted upon them the tyranny of low expectations.

They *could be* learning a valuable skill, apprenticing with a local business, learning computer programming, or perhaps traveling the world.

Instead, their brains rot in classrooms all day being exposed to boring, dry, academic theory they will never use again.

In the words of comedian Louis CK, today's youth are "non-contributing zeroes."

Okay, I'm done ranting.

The point of all this is that any "stuff" a teenager owns today was directly or indirectly purchased by their parents.

Directly, by using their own credit card to buy the item. Indirectly, by paying for nearly everything their kid could ever want or need, so that any additional income the child produces can be used exclusively for frivolous extras.

Teenagers don't do jack shit to earn what they have.

Yet teenagers judge each other based on the "stuff" they've got—as if the kid with rich parents did anything to deserve a BMW at age sixteen.

This makes no sense!

Marketing is like high school.

Remember, as adults, we are every bit as illogical as high school kids. Don't trick yourself into thinking you're much older and wiser now.

You're not.

It's just more obvious during the teen years, because the "value" conveyed by driving a nice car has absolutely *nothing* to do with what owning a BMW really says about someone (that they've been successful enough in life to afford the cost of a BMW).

Remember the example of buying a lake home earlier in the chapter?

The only reason people buy really nice houses is to show off, to make a social statement about how much money they have. I'm not knocking big houses, but it is what it is.

When someone buys a lake home, it's pretty obvious they have the means to pay for it. Banks have background checks, credit reports, and a host of other processes to make sure their loans don't end up in default.

It's pretty safe to say if someone buys a million dollar lake home, they are financially "secure."

If a sixteen-year old kid drives a BMW, it says nothing about the value he's contributed to the world. It says nothing about his skills or talents. It says nothing about how important he is or should be.

The only *logical* explanation is that his parents bought it for him. *Logically*, it should be inconsequential.

But we all know that logic takes a backseat to emotion.

High school kids will worship the kid with a BMW. They look up to kids with expensive clothes, or a cool house, as if they did anything to earn it.

Having nice stuff does not *prove* value; it only *communicates* value.

Teenagers make snap judgments based on the clothes their peers wear, the cars they drive, and the houses they live in. This continues into adulthood. How else could you explain 10,000 square foot houses?!

Most small business owners have the opposite problem: they actually provide real value, but completely fail to communicate it in a meaningful and compelling way.

I've heard the same sob story a dozen times from clients that want to work with me….

"I'm really good at what I do. I'm the best real estate agent in town. Really, I am! I'm honest, hardworking, and ethical. But I'm not making any money. That jerk across town is really good at marketing. He gets all the clients, and makes really good money. But he's a terrible agent!"

Marketing is like high school.

The money you get paid to do what you do has nothing

to do with how skilled you are at your profession.

It has *zero* correlation.

None. Nada. Zip.

It has *everything* to do with how savvy you are at marketing yourself.

Reread the previous paragraph about ten times until it starts to sink in.

Marketing is like high school; people will judge you by the value you communicate, not the value you actually provide.

Now, I'm not saying you can become a wizard at marketing but provide shitty products or services. That won't work. I'm making the assumption here that you're competent at what you do (that's the price of entry).

Beyond basic competence, don't waste time or energy trying to be the "best" in your field. It won't matter. What you should focus on is becoming the best at *marketing* in your field.

THAT is what will guarantee you retire early, rich, and happy.

Assuming you want happy clients and a ridiculously high income....

- Don't be the best massage therapist in your town. Be the best marketer of massage therapy services.

- Don't be the best insurance agent in your town. Be the best marketer of insurance products.
- Don't be the best car dealership in your town. Be the best marketer of vehicles.
- Don't be the best carpet cleaner in your town. Be the best marketer of carpet cleaning services.

You get the idea.

Making the mental leap from focusing on your deliverables to marketing those deliverables is a truly life changing, and income changing, paradigm shift. Once you grasp the importance of this principle, your business will never be the same.

It might not make sense at first, but trust me on this one! If you implement this principle in your business, you'll notice it in your bank account.   Additional zeroes are hard to miss.

We're illogical creatures, us humans. We like to think we are rational. We like to think we aren't judgmental. We like to think we value people for who they are, not what they have. We like to think that high school was a long time ago, and things are different now.

They are not.

Marketing is like high school.

Idea Nine: Marketing Is Like College

Now that you've graduated high school and moved on to bigger and better things, it's only natural for us to continue our marketing education together.....at college.

The question is whether you'll actually show up for class.

When kids ship off to college every fall, they are getting their first taste of the "real world." Well, sort of.

They're certainly more independent than they were in high school.

They have no parents telling them what time to be home by. No grades for attendance. No bells signaling them to head to their next class.

For the most part, the academic experience at college is much more open-ended and flexible than high school is. There are more "electives," and attendance itself is voluntary.

One of the indirect benefits of the higher education experience is that for most students, it's the first time in their lives they've had the opportunity to prioritize what is and isn't important to them.

Prior to college, they didn't really have a choice. They

were required, by law, to attend school for seven hours every day.

College isn't like that.

Most of the academic fare served on college campuses is voluntary. You have to *want to* attend class. You have to *want to* succeed. It's a taste of the real world.

Marketing is like college.

Never, ever, ever take your customers for granted.

No one is forcing them to buy from you. They won't face punishment from the authorities if they jump ship and take their loyalty elsewhere.

In college, and in life, you have to earn what you get.

Don't take this for granted, not for a second.

We can probably all look back at high school teachers or college professors who didn't give a shit about their job. They just showed up every day, went through the motions, and kept coming back year after year until they were granted tenure.

These were the professors that taught to empty rooms during their 8 AM classes (unless they were teaching core curriculum, that is).

On the other hand, you've probably had a few teachers throughout your life that were absolutely exceptional. You looked forward to their classes, even if they were at 7:30 in the morning.

These teachers understood that they weren't entitled to the attention and interest of their students. They had to earn it.

They had to deliver real value.

These teachers sparked in you a curiosity about the subject matter, and perhaps more importantly, a true love of learning itself.

For me, these teachers include Lyle Hovland and Amy Grussing (Willmar High School), among many others.

I wouldn't have dreamt about skipping their classes back in high school. I legitimately enjoyed their lectures, homework, and projects.

Would your customers say the same thing about your business?

Remember: in college, you don't have to show up for classes. You can stay out late partying, sleep through all your classes, and maybe still manage to scrape by with passing grades.

There are plenty of other more exciting things you could do at age 21 than park yourself in a library cubicle and study for a final. But if the teacher has done a good job communicating the value of the curriculum, you will *want to* study. You will *want to* do well.

You will actually enjoy it.

You might even tell your friends to take the class next semester (what we marketers call a *referral*).

Marketing is like college.

Never forget that your customers have more options than ever. Especially in the age of the Internet, you cannot pretend that your business exists in a vacuum.

You need to continually educate your customers, inspire them, and provide such a remarkable experience that they value what you offer over every other option available to them—including doing nothing.

This is a wonderful question to ask yourself when figuring out your business's USP, or unique selling proposition: **why should my customer choose to do business with me over any other option available to them....*including doing nothing*?**

The truth is that most small businesses cannot answer this question.

While they would never admit it, they feel entitled to their customers (yet it's the big-box retailers that are accused of not caring about their customers).

Most small businesses hide behind vague, meaningless promises like "quality, customer service, and honesty."

Guess what?

Having a quality product, decent customer service, and being honest with your customers is a pretty damn low bar to aim for. In fact, it should be the price of entry.

When all that you can come up with to differentiate your business is that you "care about the customer," you're in trouble.

Do you think other companies advertise, "We treat our customers like shit"?

That somehow if you can manage to not offend your customers by lying or cheating them, you get to brag about it?

Bragging about your customer service is a sign of weakness; specifically, it's a giveaway that you don't have anything else to actually brag about. No unique value to communicate.

You're just a commodity.

Rather than priding yourself on consistently meeting minimum expectations, what if you based your business around something unique?

Remember: customers will price shop when you don't

give them a reason not to.

It is *not* human nature to price shop. It is not a default behavior. Most people are not looking for the lowest price; they are looking for the highest value.

And those are not synonyms.

In a world where your customers can Google you, find you on Facebook, or read reviews on Yelp, it is essential that you clearly communicate your small business's unique value.

Let's break that down into two parts:

- Clear communication
- Unique value

First, it is important that the level of your communication matches the level of your contribution. If you have great products/great service, but your marketing weakly communicates this, it is no better than having poor products or service.

As in direct mail, the first step is get the customer to open the envelope. The first step is to get the prospect to give you a chance. If you have weak communication (marketing), your products will never be given the opportunity to prove themselves. You will be beaten by competition with better marketing.

Period.

And this is hard to swallow for most entrepreneurs: *the business with the best marketing, wins.*

Employment Plus (a locally owned staffing service) used to have this problem. They had the best reputation of all the recruiting firms in their area, but they didn't know how to differentiate themselves from the other agencies.

Their "product" was superior, but their marketing didn't reflect it.

And they were struggling to attract enough applicants to satisfy all of the job orders. In the staffing service, you won't be around long if you cannot send qualified candidates to your client companies.

So they decided to make a big change to their marketing strategy. Rather than advertising in the classifieds and online job boards, they decided to publish a free report.

This report promised to reveal all of the high paying jobs available in the area, and give insider information about the job-hunting process.

As you can probably imagine, this report appealed to anyone wanting or needing a new job.

It was an *irresistible offer* of valuable information.

In less than a week, Employment Plus received over 130 requests for this report (with a simple $150 ad on social media).

This is the power of measurable marketing!

All things being equal, having a good product or service is not enough. It cannot, and will not, overcome mediocre marketing.

Unless your product is so horrible that it's actually remarkably bad (in the literal sense of "worth remarking about"), a mediocre product with good marketing will ALWAYS outsell a good product with mediocre marketing.

Let that sink in.

It's incredibly difficult (some would say impossible) for organic word of mouth alone to fuel a business. Yet that is exactly what most small business owners are counting on!

Imagine you just opened an Italian restaurant. There is already a fair amount of competition in that niche from chains like Olive Garden, Macaroni Grill, etc. To stand out, it will be very difficult to rely on the quality and taste of your pasta, alfredo sauce, spaghetti, etc.

Of course, you should not serve mediocre food. If you

are not absolutely *passionate* about Italian cuisine, you should NOT open a restaurant in the first place (anyone that's ever owned a restaurant can tell you it's one of the hardest jobs in the world).

But that's a given.

Is your food really so good that you will realistically steal regional market share from Olive Garden or Macaroni Grill?

Probably not.

And I don't mean to be pessimistic; I'm simply pointing out that it's highly unlikely that your food is *so good* that people are voluntarily going door-to-door to spread the good news about your amazing breadsticks.

The breadsticks are probably good. But let's be real: they're not *that good.*

Rather than relying on word of mouth, take control of your own destiny.

Learn to be a *marketer*, not a manager.

Depending on word of mouth, organic referrals, and "buzz" will only frustrate and ultimately discourage you. It puts you at the mercy of circumstances.

However, making a conscious choice to study marketing puts you in control.

Success is a choice.

And we always have the power to choose.

But so do our customers.

They can choose to shop here, there, or no where at all. They can choose to bring a friend, or go alone. They can choose to only shop clearance sales or BOGO offers. They can choose to gladly pay full price. They can choose to never shop with you again, or they can choose to become a "regular."

And you can choose how you will influence their decisions.

Because marketing is like college.

BONUS CHAPTER: How To Automate Your Marketing Campaigns So You Can Work Less, Make More, And Spend The Extra Time With Your Family

If you've stayed with me throughout the entire book (hopefully even taken notes), you've probably started to really think about how to create more profits in your business.

It all starts with measuring your marketing.

Once the *Main Street Marketing* strategies start to sink in....once these ideas become second nature to you...once you really truly GET IT...you'll never look at advertising the same way again.

Here's what happened to me when the marketing light bulb illuminated for the first time:

When I scanned through the local newspaper and saw ads *without* an irresistible offer, or a clear call to action, it actually **bothered me.**

Almost that same feeling you get when you see a typo, or a really obvious spelling mistake in an ad.

The same thing happened whether I saw ads on TV, or got direct mail from local businesses. When I didn't see a link to a landing page to sign up for an offer, I actually started to feel bad for those businesses.

They just didn't have a clue.

I almost wanted to call them and beg them, plead with them, to start using landing pages.

You know, actually measure their marketing.

So many of the mom n' pop shops I grew up with eventually closed their doors when the national big box stores moved to town.

It's kind of sad, actually.

And I think it's a valuable lesson---if you aren't measuring your marketing, you can survive as long as there's no competition.

But once you have to compete....it's like the tide goes back out, and everyone sees that you were swimming naked the entire time.

Or, at least your accountant does, because your costs increase and your sales slow down. Sometimes it happens really slowly, over time. But sometimes it happens in a matter of weeks or months.

Because if you run your business like a hobby—something you do for fun, without real systems—without measuring your marketing—you will eventually be put out of business by someone that DOES measure their marketing.

Hindsight is 20-20.

The local businesses I remember from my childhood that aren't there anymore...if only they had read this book, if only they had taken action on the ideas.....they might still be around.

They probably just assumed that it was impossible.

But remember, David *beat* Goliath. By fighting smarter. Not harder.

You know, these local businesses, they didn't realize it, but it was completely a **marketing problem**!

Usually, the small businesses, whether they were realtors, café's, clothing stores, car dealers...you name it....usually they actually had really great service.

You know, service with a smile. And very high quality products.

They weren't selling crap. They had too much integrity to carry cheap products.

But they had too *pride* to admit they needed help with marketing.

And THAT describes most locally owned, brick n mortar, Main Street small businesses: *they have good products and poor marketing.*

Their marketing just didn't evolve with the times. And THAT is what caused their slow demise. Today, my hometown has very few local businesses that are really, truly thriving.

And if only they had known how simple the problem was. And how simple it would have been...*to solve that problem.*

Not measuring their marketing, not knowing their numbers..... it was costing them SO. MUCH. MONEY.

Hundreds, probably thousands of dollars, poured down the drain of ignorant advertising.

Money that could have been used to send their kids to college. To give more to their churches or charities. To take more family vacations while the kids were still at home.

The stuff that really matters in life.

And I'm sure they were probably frustrated. They knew something wasn't right. But even though their advertising wasn't producing any *measurable* results—whatsoever—they kept buying ads!!

Why?

Well, I think it's because we've been brainwashed over time. As entrepreneurs, we've been guilted into the idea that we need to advertise and market ourselves---even if it's not working.

For some reason, we need to "get our name out there." Even if thousands of dollars later, there is no measurable increase in business. And you probably know exactly what I'm talking about. You feel guilty if you stop running at least SOME advertising...guilty, because you know, deep down, you should be doing SOMETHING to promote your business.

There's an old saying that can be traced back to the *Mad Men* era of advertising in the 1950's....."I know half of my advertising is working. I'm just not sure which half."

And that perfectly sums up the guilt most of us feel about our advertising. We have no idea if it's working...but we keep doing it. Because we feel like abandoning advertising is somehow abandoning the business, entirely.

We've been told that we need to advertise.

And intuitively, it makes sense. So we keep spending hundreds of dollars a month on marketing that does not work.

But the worst part is, we have no way of measuring it. We have no idea what half of our advertising is working. Or more importantly, isn't working.

It's random. It's based on nothing but pure luck.

Every time we spend money on advertising, it's like playing a slot machine. And the casino always wins.

What if there was a better way?

What if you start ***measuring*** your marketing....today. Not next month, not next week.

Today.

Ultimately, what you need is a system. A marketing system that runs without you. A marketing system that is automated. And most importantly, a marketing system *that accurately measures your advertising.*

Can you honestly say that the last time you spent $200 on a newspaper ad (or radio, direct mail, etc) you knew EXACTLY to the penny what your return on investment was for that $200 advertisement?

How much new revenue did that advertisement create?

$500?

$782?

$43?

$0?

Here's the bottom line: until you can accurately measure the effectiveness of your advertising, it will be impossible to grow your business.

Not just difficult or stressful...impossible.

So that's the *bad* news—but here's the good news: small business marketing software can do all of this for you.

You don't need to bury yourself in a confusing pile of Post-It notes, redeemed coupons, or spreadsheets.

Measuring your marketing is actually pretty simple.

Imagine how easy it would be to grow your company if you knew that every time you spent $100 on an ad, it brought in $600 of new business?

How powerful would you feel if you knew that every dollar spent created six new dollars of sales?

I mean, really, stop and think about that...

How powerful would you *feel?*

It would change everything!!! If you wanted to increase revenues by $2,400 next month, all you would need to do is invest $400 in measurable ads.

So here's the question....why wait?

What if you created a new ad as soon as you finished reading this...an ad you could actually measure?

What if you created your first landing page, spent $100 on a small newspaper ad, and got 14 brand new leads. What if easy-to-use software kept track of everything for you, so you knew that your *Cost Per Lead* was exactly $7.14?

$100 divided by 14.

And if what if it took you less than 5 minutes to set this up?

If it only took you 5 minutes to create this system, would you have any reason *not to* start measuring your marketing?

What if this software was so easy to use, your frontline employees making $8/hour could manage *all of this for you.*

Imagine how it would feel to know that you can actually measure your ads—that for the first time, you are in control.

Because you can *measure* everything.

And because you can measure, you can IMPROVE your numbers.

You can GROW your business.

I want to give you the opportunity of a lifetime.

And I really mean that.

FrontDesk marketing software has the power to completely transform your small business….today.

Right now.

FrontDesk was designed to transform small business marketing from being stressful, random, and frustrating, to being simple, measurable, and profitable.

What sounds better to you?

Stressful, random, and frustrating.....or simple, measurable, and profitable?

It's a choice you make.

And up until this point, it's a choice *you have been making*. Where your small business is right now is the result of the choices you have made up until this point.

Are you happy with where things are? Or are you stressed, overworked, and a little frustrated?

(Usually the stress and frustration of running a small business has nothing to do with profits or revenues, it actually stems from *not knowing what to do*, the feeling of not being in control.)

That might be the most important thing to remember!

Choosing to simplify your life is a *decision*.

- You are not a victim of the economy.

- You are not a victim of competition from online retailers.

- You are not a victim of external circumstances.

You can choose to keep doing what you're doing, or you can choose to simplify your life. You can choose to own your business, instead of it owning you. You can choose to have more time with your family.

What will you choose?

Big companies typically employ entire teams of employees to measure and manage the marketing. But you don't have to invest hundreds of thousands of dollars every year on a marketing team.

Simplifying your business isn't expensive.

You don't have to invest $60,000 to hire a marketing manager.

You don't have to spend $6,000....or even $600.

Remember: simplifying your life is a choice.

What's your freedom worth to you?

What's your time worth to you?

What's your family worth to you?

Is it worth more than $32/month?

The answer is entirely up to you.

Being a small business owner is a noble calling. Most people will never understand what goes on behind the scenes! Even if you tried to explain it to them, they wouldn't get it. *As an entrepreneur, you are part of an elite minority of visionaries.*

Never forget that.

But it shouldn't require 80 hours a week, credit card debt, and being away from your family on nights and weekends.

It's time to stop bragging about working so hard, like it's some sort of entrepreneurial badge of honor. Let's be honest with ourselves: we deserve better than this.

Our families deserve better than this.

If you have kids, *they* deserve better than this.

Do you attend every one of your son or daughter's dance recitals, baseball games, or band concerts?

How many have you missed?

Remember...it's a choice.

But it doesn't have to be this way.

Would you invest $32/month to take your life back? To own your small business, instead of it owning you?

Would you invest $32/month if it meant seeing your wife and kids more often?

Is seeing all of your son's Little League games, or his varsity football season....worth $32/month?

How about your daughter's volleyball games, or her dance recitals? Is that worth $32/month to you?

How often do you get to see your wife? Or your husband? Is it worth $32/month to free up the time to go on more dates?

How many times in the last month have you taken your spouse out for dinner and a movie?

Is that even *possible* right now?

Choosing to simplify your life starts with taking control of your small business. And that means taking control of the marketing.

But it won't happen randomly or by accident. You will have to choose!

So here's the question: If measuring your marketing resulted in another $20,000 this year (or more), what would that mean for your business?

For your family?

Here's an even better question...

What's it costing you to *not* measure your marketing?

Let's get specific, and talk about the marketing math: do you think it's worth it to invest $32/month to help your business create *tens of thousands in extra profits*?

Maybe even hundreds of thousands?

With FrontDesk software, marketing is simple. As it should be.

And it's just $32/month.

But you'll have to make a decision. Taking back your life won't happen randomly, by accident. Your small business will not simplify itself. You will need to make a choice.

And I want to make this the easiest decision you've ever made.

You can start measuring your marketing today...for FREE.

Use the coupon code I'll give you in a moment, and you can start using FrontDesk marketing software for FREE.

Normally, there is a $97 activation fee. But not today.

Not now.

You can get started right away creating measurable marketing campaigns by using the coupon code: MSMBOOK

Just go to www.tryfrontdesk.com and sign up for an account. It's really that easy! Use the coupon code MSMBOOK to get started for free.

It's a simple decision to make. But it could change your life, forever.

What's it costing you to *not* get started?

What's it costing you to *not* act?

What's it costing you to *not* measure your marketing?

Life is a series of decisions.

How many more baseball games or dance recitals will you *choose* to miss?

Usually we overcomplicate things to avoid taking any responsibility for our lives. But being an entrepreneur is about taking risks, and being willing to make the hard decisions that most people are not willing to make.

Our employees take a paycheck. We'd rather *create* one.

So don't accept the lie that being an entrepreneur means you have to compromise in other areas of your life. The "pride" of owning a small business is not adequate compensation for ignoring your children.

Or your marriage.

.   That's not a fair trade. Not fair for you, but especially not fair for your family.

It's time to make a decision.

Will you choose to keep doing what you're doing?

Will you choose to continue managing a business that is stressful, random, and frustrating?

Or would you rather manage a business that is simple, measurable, and profitable?

Do you want to own your business, or let it own you?

Be honest with yourself—*it will be very easy to set this book down, forget about it, and pretend that everything is fine.*

That would be the easy thing to do.

What I've found is that the hardest part about measuring your marketing is making a choice to *begin* measuring your marketing.

It's time to make a decision.

FrontDesk software is easy to use. It takes less than five minutes to create a campaign. The hardest part about measuring your marketing is *choosing to get started.*

So I want to make that decision as easy as possible!

Sign up using the special coupon code MSMBOOK, and you can get started immediately creating measurable marketing campaigns.

You won't pay a penny.

With FrontDesk you can immediately generate more customers and more profits in your business, by creating measurable marketing campaigns with custom landing pages and automated follow up.

It's time to measure your marketing!

And you can get started TODAY. Right now.

I can personally guarantee you that no program is as EASY to use as FrontDesk.

It's simple.

It's beautiful.

"Learning" how to use FrontDesk takes less than five minutes!

So get started, today. Don't wait.

FrontDesk is priced so that *any small business, in any industry, in any circumstance, can afford it.*

It's only $32/month after your first month....which is free with the coupon code in this book.

So don't wait any longer. Visit www.tryfrontdesk.com, and enter the coupon code MSMBOOK.

Don't keep crossing your fingers, hoping, praying your business will improve.

There's a better way....

Get started measuring your marketing. TODAY. For free.

Your small business, and your bank account, will never be the same.

Made in the USA
Charleston, SC
25 September 2014